I0086287

Solving *the* Money Puzzle

God's Plan for Financial Freedom

MIKE COE

Copyright © 2013 Mike Coe

"Teaching the practical applications to Biblical principles"

All rights reserved, including the right to reproduce this book or portions thereof in any form whatsoever without the prior written permission of the author.

ISBN-13: 978-0615938547

PRINTED IN THE UNITED STATES OF AMERICA

Coebooks.com

Scripture quotations noted KJV are taken from the King James Version.

Scripture quotations noted NIV are taken from the Holy Bible, New International Version®, NIV® Copyright © 1973, 1978, 1984, 2011 by Biblica, Inc.® Used by permission. All rights reserved worldwide.

Scripture quotations marked (NLT) are taken from the Holy Bible, New Living Translation, copyright © 1996, 2004, 2007 by Tyndale House Foundation. Used by permission of Tyndale House Publishers, Inc., Carol Stream, Illinois 60188. All rights reserved.

Scripture (marked GW) is taken from GOD'S WORD®, © 1995 God's Word to the Nations. Used by permission of Baker Publishing Group.

Scripture taken from *The Message*. Copyright © 1993, 1994, 1995, 1996, 2000, 2001, 2002. Used by permission of NavPress Publishing Group.

Scripture quotations taken from the Amplified® Bible, Copyright © 1954, 1958, 1962, 1964, 1965, 1987 by The Lockman Foundation Used by permission." (www.Lockman.org)

Scripture quotations marked (GNT) are from the Good News Translation in Today's English Version- Second Edition Copyright © 1992 by American Bible Society. Used by Permission.

Scripture quotations marked (ERV) are taken from the Holy Bible: Easy-To-Read © 2001, 2006 by World Bible Translation Center, Inc. and used by permission.

"The earth is the Lord's, and everything in it, the world, and all who live in it."

(Psalm 24:1 NIV)

CONTENTS

Introduction

Nearly twenty-five years ago, while I was driving home from work, I cried out to God, "Lord, how do I fix the financial mess that I have created?"

I knew that once I arrived home and joined my wife and two young children, the conversation I was having with God would need to be postponed. I couldn't wait another day…another hour…another minute! I pulled into a bank parking lot.

While sitting alone in my car, I sensed God's presence. It was a peaceful feeling that calmed my troubled heart. I was pretty sure God knew what I was thinking before I even prayed, but I needed to verbalize my thoughts. It was my way of acknowledging my surrender to His will.

I prayed, "God, you know my situation. I have a money problem. I need your guidance. What should I do?"

He replied, *It's not about the money!*

I prayed, "Lord, I'll do anything."

He said, *Get out of debt.*

I said, "What do I do first?"

He said, *Sell your house.*

Selling the house might have seemed a bit extreme, but I knew it was the step of faith I needed to take. At the time, the house we were living in was far more than we could afford. The first thought that hit me was… *What will my wife say? She loves our home. How can I expect her to agree to take such a drastic step?*

So I asked God. "Lord, if this is what you want me to do, my wife needs to be on board. In some way, you have to tell her what you have told me. You have to work a miracle."

I drove home, ate dinner with my family, then cleaned up the kitchen while my wife helped the children get ready for bed.

Once the kids were settled and the house was quiet, I told my wife that we needed to talk. We sat in the den and I said, "I feel like God wants us to get out of debt."

She said, "What do you think we should do first?"

I paused, thinking she might not like what I was about to say, but I knew we couldn't pretend any longer. We needed to take aggressive action. I said, "Sell the house."

She calmly replied, "Fine, let's do it."

At that time, the housing market was horrible. Nothing was selling in our price range. Homes the size of ours had been on the market for years.

Again, I asked God, "Lord, if You are in control of selling our house, like I know You are, I will put a sign in the front yard and let You sell it."

That weekend, I put a sign in the front yard: FOR SALE BY OWNER. The house sold in one week at full price. It was a miracle!

Shortly after the house sold, my wife was at the grocery store.

She bumped into a friend and casually mentioned to the lady about our upcoming move. When asked what we were planning to do, my wife told her that we were looking for a house to rent. The woman said she had a two-bedroom rental house that had just become vacant. She offered to rent it to us for $300 per month. Another miracle!

In one of my next talks with God, I prayed, *"Lord, what you have shown me with the selling of my house has definitely increased my faith. I know you are doing this, so what do we do next?"*

He said, *"Sell your business."*

So I did.

From there, the story continued with more miracles—too many to tell in this short book. The point I would like to emphasize is that God was waiting on me before He could act. When I finally surrendered and was willing to listen, God had all the answers. He is ready to do the same for you.

Solving the Money Puzzle is a summary of the most important verses, parables, and principles that helped me understand God's design for financial freedom.

Finding financial freedom required that I first change my thinking. As a Christian, I was fully aware of God's design for my life in every area except my finances. I had heard numerous sermons and teachings on money, but every message seemed to emphasize giving, rather than living. Before I could fully understand financial freedom, I had to understand that it was *not* about the money. I know this might sound strange, but trust me, once you "get" it, you too will be instantly set free. Once the heavy weight you have been carrying is given to God, you will soar!

Sadly, the majority of families living in the top ten economies in the world (U.S., China, Japan, Germany, France, Brazil, U.K., Russia, Italy, and India)—especially the U.S.—are living paycheck-to-paycheck. One missed paycheck means the minimums due on bloated credit card bills can't be paid, or the mortgage payment will be late, or the needed maintenance on the car must be postponed indefinitely.

Imagine a row of ten houses tucked away in a typical middle-American subdivision. Statistically, two of those houses are bordered by white-picket fences with children happily playing in the front yard. The families are living responsibly within their means with adequate savings put aside for unexpected financial emergencies. The other eight families could be described by the hypothetical six o'clock news report below:

"While financial homes are burning to the ground, weary homeowners continue to boost the flames by adding staggering amounts of debt to the roaring blaze of doom. Their impulsive and irresponsible spending acts like a never-ending wind, fanning the flames."

Although you would never hear a report like that on your local evening news, it is a fact that financial chaos, like a cancer, is ravaging the lives of millions of Americans. Their cries for help often go unanswered. Marriages are destroyed, children are confused, and families are left to sift through the rubble once the flames of financial chaos have died.

Solving the Money Puzzle will show you where you can find the missing piece in the money puzzle, and how you can have true financial freedom. God's design offers a fail-safe plan that works. I highly recommend, *before* you read any books on money management and wealth building, you first read what God has to say on the subject. Over two thousand verses in the

Bible deal with money. One out of every six verses in Matthew, Mark, and Luke is about material possessions. Nearly half of Jesus' parables are about possessions. Jesus spoke more about money and how to use it than he did about heaven and hell combined.

Financial *order* and wealth building (spending less than you make) are not as elusive as most might think. Those who follow a logical step-by-step spending plan, who eliminate consumer debt, and who control emotional and impulsive spending habits can enjoy the benefits of living a fiscally responsible life. However, financial *order* and wealth building (both important) are not synonymous with, nor prerequisites for, financial *freedom*. Financial freedom is reserved for those who have gained a correct relationship with money—the most important piece of the money puzzle.

As crazy as it might sound, true financial freedom really has nothing to do with income, possessions, or wealth, but everything to do with attitude. Most of the wealthiest people in the world are slaves to their money and lack true financial freedom. Money might buy the things and experiences that bring temporary pleasure, but it can never buy the peace and contentment that are the by-products of freedom. Money and the comfort it provides will never fully satisfy: *the eyes of man are never satisfied* (Proverbs 27:20 KJV).

Solving the Money Puzzle is more about you than it is about money. Money can only do what you tell it to do. Money is neither good nor evil—it is amoral. Money can build a church or pay a prostitute. So the problem is not money. The problem is you. The Bible says: *For the love of money is a root of all kinds of evil. Some people, eager for money, have wandered from the faith and pierced themselves with many griefs* (1 Timothy 6:10 NIV).

The key words in this verse are: *the love of money.* Before you can solve the money puzzle, it is essential that you first develop a correct relationship with money. Simply put, the last and most critical piece in the money puzzle is *you.*

Solving the Money Puzzle is divided into three sections with three chapters in each section:

Section one deals with attitude (your relationship to money).

Section two deals with application (practical steps).

Section three deals with assimilation (lifestyle benefits).

Each chapter presents key Biblical principles regarding money, planning, working, giving, saving, debt, investing, teaching children about money, and relating to the government.

The main objective of this book is to equip the Christian with the Biblical knowledge and wisdom necessary to live in accordance with God's design for financial freedom.

You should live in a way that proves you belong to the God who calls you into his kingdom and glory (1 Thessalonians 2:12 GW).

After each chapter, I challenge you to ask yourself: "What do I need to change in order to put God first in my finances?"

PART ONE
Attitude

Chapter One
Financial Freedom - God's Way

Malcolm Forbes was one of the wealthiest people to have lived in our time. The billionaire publisher was the one who came up with the oft-quoted phrase, "He who dies with the most toys wins." The truth is that those who die with the most toys are just dead. Jesus said, *"Life is not measured by how much you own"* (Luke 12:15 NLT).

How do you define financial freedom? Can a Christian be wealthy and still walk in God's will? When it comes to finances, what is the difference between an owner and a manager?

The secular world defines freedom as being able to do what you want, when you want. If applied to finances, this equates to having what you want, when you want it. Webster defines being free as, *no longer burdened by obligation and debt...* Sadly, when dreams of financial freedom appear out of reach, many people turn to easy credit. One bad decision after another cause the flames of despair, regret, and hopelessness to burn out of control.

Living in a consumption-based economy doesn't make it any easier. Endless streams of advertisements promote products promising to make you feel better and find more satisfaction from life. As you cogitate on the idea of a more satisfied life, you strategize and compromise a way to justify purchasing every trinket that excites you. After purchasing the shiny new toy, you soon realize that the satisfaction was temporary and fleeting. The wisdom in God's Word warns you to be aware of such misplaced beliefs:

Whoever loves money never has enough; whoever loves wealth is never satisfied with their income (Eccl. 5:10 NIV).

The eyes of man are never satisfied (Proverbs 27:20 (b) KJV).

Don't wear yourself out trying to get rich; restrain yourself!

Riches disappear in the blink of an eye; wealth sprouts wings and flies off into the wild blue yonder (Proverbs 23:4-5 MSG).

In order to correct the misplaced belief that more money will satisfy, you must replace the thinking of secular society with the wisdom found in God's Word.

Don't misunderstand me. Wealth is not a bad thing when you have the right attitude and understand that God is the Giver of all riches and wealth. With the *right attitude*, a wealthy person can be a great blessing to the work of the Lord. However, it is a slippery slope that most people are unable to manage.

Scripture teaches that there is a great danger when one is *wanting of nothing*. Jesus used parables and illustrations to teach how self-sufficiency and independence make it extremely difficult to trust in God. It often takes a misfortune that money cannot correct before the right attitude and perspective can be acquired.

Although there are many warnings given to those that God has blessed with wealth, the Bible never says it is wrong to accumulate wealth. God is only concerned with our attitudes. Envy, hoarding, greed, and the lack of concern for the needs of others are examples of the attitudes that God warns against. Those who are obsessed with the single motive of growing wealth end up with nothing but wasted lives.

King Solomon—the wisest, richest, and most influential king in Israel's history—was, in the eyes of the world, financially free. Here is what he had to say about the riches and wealth he had been given by God:

There are people, for instance, on whom God showers everything—money, property, reputation—all they ever wanted or dreamed of. And then God doesn't let them enjoy it. Some stranger comes along and has all the fun. It's more of what I'm calling smoke. A bad business (Ecclesiastes 6:1-2 MSG).

Parable of the Rich Fool

Jesus used the *Parable of the Rich Fool* to emphasize the dangers of hoarding and greed. It serves as a warning to those who are rich and who desire to be rich.

Jesus said: *Then he said to them, "Watch out! Be on your guard against all kinds of greed; life does not consist in an abundance of possessions."*

And he told them this parable: "The ground of a certain rich man yielded an abundant harvest. He thought to himself, 'What shall I do? I have no place to store my crops.' Then he said, 'This is what I'll do. I will tear down my barns and build bigger ones, and there I will store my surplus grain. And I'll say to myself, You have plenty of grain laid up for many years. Take life easy; eat, drink and be merry.'

"But God said to him, 'You fool! This very night your life will be demanded from you. Then who will get what you have prepared for yourself?' This is how it will be with whoever stores up things for themselves but is not rich toward God" (Luke 12:15-21 NIV).

Jesus often made examples of situations where he detected an incorrect attitude. In the *Parable of the Rich Fool*, Jesus points out the vanity of the rich man's pursuits. Instead of laying up treasure for ourselves on Earth, Jesus encourages us to maintain an eternal perspective.

The Parable of the Rich Young Ruler

The *Parable of the Rich Young Ruler* is another example of one of Jesus' teachings on our attitude toward money:

One day one of the local officials asked him, "Good Teacher, what must I do to deserve eternal life?"

Jesus said, "Why are you calling me good? No one is good— only God. You know the commandments, don't you? No illicit sex, no killing, no stealing, no lying, honor your father and mother."

He said, "I've kept them all for as long as I can remember."

When Jesus heard that, he said, "Then there's only one thing left to do: Sell everything you own and give it away to the poor. You will have riches in heaven. Then come, follow me."

This was the last thing the official expected to hear. He was very rich and became terribly sad. He was holding on tight to a lot of things and not about to let them go.

Seeing his reaction, Jesus said, "Do you have any idea how difficult it is for people who have it all to enter God's kingdom? I'd say it's easier to thread a camel through a needle's eye than get a rich person into God's kingdom."

"Then who has any chance at all?" the others asked.

"No chance at all," Jesus said, "if you think you can pull it off

by yourself, (but) every chance in the world if you trust God to do it" (Luke 18:18-27 MSG).

In the *Parable of the Rich Young Ruler*, Jesus made clear how difficult it is to develop the right attitude about money and wealth. As paradoxical as it may sound, it is usually the riches and wealth of a person that robs them of financial freedom.

Jesus made it extremely clear where real freedom could be found: *Then Jesus turned to the Jews who had claimed to believe in him. "If you stick with this, living out what I tell you, you are my disciples for sure. Then you will experience for yourselves the truth, and the truth will free you"* (John 8:31-32 MSG).

Trusting in God's design for financial freedom requires that you surrender your will. It does not mean that you can now sit back and expect God to bless you with great wealth. It means that you are now ready to begin learning what your position of responsibility is as a manager rather than an owner. It means that you have truly been convinced that God's plan for your finances is in your best interest.

God wants you to partner with him in accomplishing his

purposes on Earth. God really isn't interested in watching you fulfill your dream for your life; he wants you to fulfill His dream for your life. If Christ is truly your King, then you understand that Christ's kingdom has a different set of rules, a different set of values, and a different economy. In Christ's kingdom, the purpose for earthly wealth is to invest in eternal treasures.

Do not store up for yourselves treasures on earth, where moth and rust destroy, and where thieves break in and steal. But store up for yourselves treasures in heaven, where moth and rust do not destroy, and where thieves do not break in and steal (Matthew 6:19-20 NIV).

As you transfer more and more of your trust in the area of your finances to God, you will begin to develop a new attitude about what it means to be wealthy. Anything the world has to offer pales in comparison to the reality of God's blessings: *"Truly I tell you,"* Jesus replied, *"no one who has left home or brothers or sisters or mother or father or children or fields for me and the gospel will fail to receive a hundred times as much in this present age..."* (Mark 10:29 NIV).

In your journey towards true financial freedom, the most

important truth that you as a Christian must incorporate into your attitude is that *God owns everything, and the ability to have anything is given by Him and Him alone*. Without a genuine acceptance of this one Biblical truth, the Christian can *never* be financially free. With the right attitude:

1) The poor and struggling family will continue to do all they can to improve their financial situation, yet be content with what God allows them to manage.

2) The middle class family will turn their focus on loving others and stop transferring their wealth to banks in the form of interest payments on borrowed money.

3) The wealthy family will begin to see their wealth as a great responsibility and resource for the Kingdom and start trusting in God rather than their riches.

God Made It All.

Through him all things were made; without him nothing was made that has been made (John 1:3 NIV).

For in him all things were created: things in heaven and on earth, visible and invisible, whether thrones or powers or rulers

21

or authorities; all things have been created through him and for him (Colossians 1:16 NIV).

Rich and poor have this in common: The Lord is the Maker of them all (Proverbs 22:2 NIV).

God Owns It All.

Look around you: Everything you see is God's—the heavens above and beyond, the Earth, and everything on it (Deuteronomy 10:14 MSG).

Yours,Lord, is the greatness and the power and the glory and the majesty and the splendor, for everything in heaven and earth is yours (1 Chronicles 29:11 NIV).

For every animal of the forest is mine, and the cattle on a thousand hills. I know every bird in the mountains, and the insects in the fields are mine. If I were hungry I would not tell you, for the world is mine, and all that is in it (Psalms 50:10-12 NIV).

The earth is the Lord's, and everything in it, the world, and all who live in it (Psalm 24:1 NIV).

"The silver is mine and the gold is mine," declares the Lord

Almighty (Haggai 2:8 NIV).

God Owns You.

You are not your own. You are special to God. He made you and shaped you in your mother's womb for a very special purpose: *God decided to give you life through the word of truth so you might be the most important of all the things he made* (James 1:18 NIV).

At birth, you become responsible to God. The Bible teaches that life on this earth can be orderly and meaningful only insofar as there is a clear understanding of your relationship to God (God is sovereign and man is subject to God).

It's in Christ that you find out who you are and what you are living for. Long before you first heard of Christ and got your hopes up, he had his eye on you, had designs on you for glorious living, part of the overall purpose he is working out in everything and everyone (Ephesians 1:11-12 MSG).

You are not your own; you were bought at a price (1 Corinthians 6:19b-20a NIV).

God owns your body, soul, mind and talents. Your refusal to

accept God's ownership takes you out of His will.

The Parable of the Talents

In the *Parable of the Talents,* Jesus teaches what it means to be a manager of what God has entrusted.

"It's also like a man going off on an extended trip. He called his servants together and delegated responsibilities. To one he gave five thousand dollars, to another two thousand, to a third one thousand, depending on their abilities. Then he left. Right off, the first servant went to work and doubled his master's investment. The second did the same. But the man with the single thousand dug a hole and carefully buried his master's money.

"After a long absence, the master of those three servants came back and settled up with them. The one given five thousand dollars showed him how he had doubled his investment. His master commended him: 'Good work! You did your job well. From now on be my partner.'

"The servant with the two thousand showed how he also had doubled his master's investment. His master commended him: 'Good work! You did your job well. From now on be my

24

partner.'

"The servant given one thousand said, 'Master, I know you have high standards and hate careless ways, that you demand the best and make no allowances for error. I was afraid I might disappoint you, so I found a good hiding place and secured your money. Here it is, safe and sound down to the last cent.'

"The master was furious. 'That's a terrible way to live! It's criminal to live cautiously like that! If you knew I was after the best, why did you do less than the least? The least you could have done would have been to invest the sum with the bankers, where at least I would have gotten a little interest.

"'Take the thousand and give it to the one who risked the most. And get rid of this "play-it-safe" who won't go out on a limb. Throw him out into utter darkness.' (Matthew 24:14-30 MSG).

God owns it all, even you! You own nothing! You are only a manager (steward) of what God has given you. Webster's dictionary defines a "steward" as *one who manages another's property.* God decides what you are to manage based on your abilities (both God given and acquired). Just as with the servants in the parable, God is concerned with your attitude and your motives rather than the money itself.

Although the first two servants received different amounts of money to manage, their rewards were the same. After the master had seen what they had done, his response was the same to both of them: *"Good work! You did your job well. From now on be my partner."* Because of their faith, they could now be entrusted with more responsibility. They were then told that they could now *"...enter thou into the joy of thy lord."* This shows that the amount of money was not important. What was important was that both servants had the right attitude and did the best they could with what they had been given.

The *Parable of the Talents* shows that God is pleased when you acknowledge His total ownership and accept your appointed position as a steward (manager). Financial freedom is not about the money, it's about your attitude—your relationship with the money. God made everything and God owns everything—even you. You are the manager of what God chooses to give you to manage according to your abilities. Once you embrace this concept, you are ready to move on to the next chapter: *The Battle for Freedom.*

Chapter Two
The Battle for Freedom

Why is the love of money the root of all kinds of evil? In a world dominated by secular reasoning, where truth is relative, how can we know what is true? What does it mean to have the fear of God?

There is a great battle raging inside of every Christian. This battle is between your inherited sinful nature (Romans 5:12; Psalm 51:5) and the Holy Spirit (Galatians 5:16, 17).

In addition, you are at war against the forces of darkness and wickedness in the world around you: *For our struggle is not against flesh and blood, but against the rulers, against the authorities, against the powers of this dark world and against the spiritual forces of evil in the heavenly realms* (Ephesians 6:12 NIV). You are fighting for your freedom!

One of the greatest weapons of the enemy is your love of money. It is not about the money, but your relationship to the money—your *love* of the money: *Whoever loves money never has enough; whoever loves wealth is never satisfied with their income* (Ecclesiastes 5:10 NIV).

In the Sermon on the Mount, Jesus said, *"No one can serve two masters. Either you will hate the one and love the other, or you will be devoted to the one and despise the other. You cannot serve both God and money"* (Matthew 6:24 NIV).

Jesus likens a *love of money* to idolatry. He refers to money as a *master* we serve at the expense of serving God. We are commanded by God to have *no other gods* before the only true and living God. (Exodus 20:3 NIV; the first commandment).

Every day, you are attacked from every side in hopes of getting you to succumb to your inner desires. You are told that you will never feel complete unless every want and desire is met. You are told that satisfying these cravings will bring you happiness and peace. You are also told that *more* is better and *new* is best, regardless of the price or sacrifice required to obtain it. Over the years, you have become a master of compromise and a genius at justifying the trinkets, gadgets, and pleasures of life. *Out with the old and in with the new and much improved* has become the motto of our consumption-based society.

The love of money, and the comforts it buys, is as powerful as any mind-altering drug. Like termites, this craving slowly eats away at your financial house. Poor planning, greed, hoarding, impulsive buying, jealousy, waste, and debt rob you of your freedom. But worse than a hoard of termites eating the foundation of your financial house, the love of money is slowly destroying relationships and luring you into a purposeless and hopeless life.

Winning the Battle

The good news is the battle can be won and financial freedom can be yours! Once you adopt God's attitude in place of the attitude of our broken and wayward society, you will find freedom and peace. I like to think of it as a two-step process.

Step 1: Understanding Truth and Where to Find It

Then Jesus turned to the Jews who had claimed to believe in him. *"If you stick with this, living out what I tell you, you are my disciples for sure. Then you will experience for yourselves the truth, and the truth will free you"* (John 8:30-32 MSG).

God's divine strategy for the Christian is found in the words of Jesus. His attitudes about life should become our absolutes. When you understand the truth He represents, you will find freedom. *Jesus answered, "I am the way and the truth and the life..."* (John 14:6 NIV).

Paul wrote: *Christ has set us free to live a free life. So take your stand! Never again let anyone put a harness of slavery on you* (Galatians 5:1 MSG).

It is your choice. You can find truth and freedom in Christ, or be enslaved to the secular belief that truth is relative and financial freedom is found through abundance.

Jesus promised that He would send the Holy Spirit to guide you and help you distinguish what is true and what is false: *"But when he, the Spirit of truth, comes, he will guide you into all the truth"* (John 16:13(a) NIV).

Every Christian has the Holy Spirit living within them. It is the same Holy Spirit that resurrected Christ from the grave: *The*

Spirit of truth. The world cannot accept him, because it neither sees him nor knows him. But you know him, for he lives with you and will be in you (John 14:17 NIV). It is through the help of the Holy Spirit that you grow to understand God's attitude and His truths.

With a pure heart (confessed of all sin), when you study the principles found in God's Word, the Holy Spirit takes the knowledge in your head and plants it firmly within your heart. With a pure heart, you are able to make decisions and choices that will lead you to a life of freedom, joy, and peace.

Equipped with truth, the Christian is given the opportunity to win the battle for freedom and be set free from the things that enslave most people on this earth. This great benefit can be enjoyed by developing the attitude of Christ which allows you to recognize the truth.

But you belong to God, my dear children. You have already won a victory over those people, because the Spirit who lives in you is greater than the spirit who lives in the world. Those people belong to this world, so they speak from the world's viewpoint, and the world listens to them. But we belong to God, and those who know God listen to us. If they do not belong to

God, they do not listen to us. That is how we know if someone has the Spirit of truth or the spirit of deception (1 John 4:4-6 NLT).

Step 2: Knowing and Fearing the Lord

The further you distance yourself from God, the less you fear Him. The less you fear Him, the less you are willing to acknowledge your need to know His truth. Without His truth, you will live a defeated Christian life. Conversely, the closer you draw yourself to Him, the better you will know Him. The better you know Him, the more you will fear Him and subsequently recognize the need to know and apply His truth in your life. If you truly know Him, you will want to obey His principles and abide by His instructions. This includes handling your money.

And we can be sure that we know him if we obey his commandments. If someone claims, "I know God," but doesn't obey God's commandments, that person is a liar and is not living in the truth. But those who obey God's word truly show how completely they love him. That is how we know we are living in him. Those who say they live in God should live their lives as Jesus did (1 John 2:3-6 NLT).

They claim to know God, but by their actions they deny him. They are detestable, disobedient and unfit for doing anything good (Titus 1:16 NIV).

You learn to know *about* God as you read and study His Word. You learn to *know* God when you start depending on Him in every area of life. This results in the development of your prayer life. The more you see Him work in your life; the more you know and understand Him. The more you know and understand Him, the more you fear Him. A healthy fear of the Lord is your most powerful weapon in your battle for freedom.

For the unbeliever, the fear of God is the fear of the judgment of God and eternal death (eternal separation from God). *But I will show you whom you should fear: Fear him who, after your body has been killed, has authority to throw you into hell. Yes, I tell you, fear him* (Luke 12:5 NIV).

It is a fearful thing to fall into the hands of the living God (Hebrews 10:31 NIV).

Until you understand who God is and develop a reverential fear of Him, you cannot have true wisdom. True wisdom comes only from understanding who God is and that He is holy, just, and righteous.

Spend a few minutes and meditate on the following verses:

The fear of the Lord is the beginning of knowledge, but fools despise wisdom and instruction (Proverbs 1:7 NIV).

The fear of the Lord is the beginning of wisdom, and knowledge of the Holy One is understanding (Proverbs 9:10 NIV).

The fear of the Lord adds length to life, but the years of the wicked are cut short (Proverbs 10:27 NIV).

The fear-of God builds up confidence, and makes a world safe for your children (Proverbs 14:26 MSG).

The fear of the Lord is a fountain of life, turning a person from the snares of death (Proverbs 14:27 NIV).

Through love and faithfulness sin is atoned for; through the fear of the LORD evil is avoided (Proverbs 16:6 (NIV).

The fear of the Lord leads to life; then one rests content, untouched by trouble (Proverbs 19:23 NIV).

Blessed is the one who always trembles before God, but whoever hardens their heart falls into trouble (Proverbs 28:14 NIV).

Fear the Lord, you his holy people, for those who fear him lack nothing (Psalm 34:9 NIV).

Blessed are those who fear the Lord, who find great delight in his commands. Their children will be mighty in the land; the generation of the upright will be blessed. Wealth and riches are in their houses, and their righteousness endures forever (Psalm 112:1-3 NIV).

Fearing the Lord is the greatest deterrent to living a self-absorbed life. When you truly believe that God is aware of every decision and choice you make, you will think more carefully before you act.

Listed below are a few of the benefits (taken from the verses above) of knowing God and fearing Him: *knowledge, wisdom, understanding, long life, confidence, keeps our children safe, avoid evil, rest, contentment, untouched by trouble, lacking nothing, produces children that are leaders and generations that are blessed, brings wealth and riches into our homes.*

A life freed from the worries of finances, or any other issue, begins when you get to know God and fear Him. The more you know Him, the greater your desire will be to live your life according to the truth found in His Word. To know what to do and not do it will keep you living a life filled with fear, worry, regret, and failure. *If anyone, then, knows the good they ought to do and doesn't do it, it is sin for them* (James 4:17 NIV).

Even when you know what to do, it's not easy. Our materialistic world has a never ending supply of ammunition for the enemy to use to tempt you. There is something for everyone. Jesus warned his disciples about how easy it is to be taken over by temptation: *"Watch and pray so that you will not fall into temptation. The spirit is willing, but the flesh is weak"* (Matthew 26:41 NIV).

In the *Parable of the Sower*, Jesus explained how the world chokes the seed of Truth from producing fruit: *As for what was sown among thorns, this is he who hears the Word, but the cares of the world and the pleasure and delight and glamour and deceitfulness of riches choke and suffocate the Word, and it yields not fruit* (Matthew 13:22 AMP).

In effect, it is impossible for you to win the battle alone. God knows this. That is why He sent his Son to die on the cross for you. He then sent the Holy Spirit to live inside you and guide you through every choice. On top of that, He gave you His Words in a Book, the Bible. Filled with truth and wisdom, the Bible will answer your many questions and instruct you how to be successful in the practical affairs of everyday life. He knew that you couldn't do it alone.

To win the battle, you must desire to surrender your life to His will. You must be quick to confess your sins. You must ask the Holy Spirit to fill your life and teach you truth. You must read the Bible and become familiar with God's attitude toward life. When you surrender your life to God's ways instead of yours, you will find freedom. You will learn how to become a better manager of all of the areas of your life. When this happens, the battle for freedom has been won!

Chapter Three
God's Perspective on Work

"No one should ever work. Work is the source of nearly all the misery in the world. Almost any evil you'd care to name comes from working or from living in a world designed for work. In order to stop suffering, we have to stop working." These are the words of Bob Black in 1985 from his essay, *The Abolition of Work.*

What does the Bible say about work? Is work a curse, or is it something that humans were uniquely designed to do? What should your attitude be in regard to your work?

Many Christians believe that when God first created man, he

was not required to work. Many believe that the man was put in the Garden of Eden and that all he had to do was sit back and take it easy for the rest of eternity. Then, one day God saw that the man was bored, so to make things even better for the man, God made a beautiful woman to give him company. This is far from the truth.

God created man in His image with characteristics like Him. He created man to work with Him in the world. *Now the Lord God had planted a garden in the east, in Eden; and there he put the man he had formed* (Genesis 2:8 NIV).

From the first day that God put Adam in the Garden of Eden, he was given a job. *The Lord God took the man and put him in the Garden of Eden to work it and take care of it* (Genesis 2:15 NIV). It was a partnership.

Another job God gave man was the job of naming all the animals. *Now the Lord God had formed out of the ground all the wild animals and all the birds in the sky. He brought them to the man to see what he would name them; and whatever the man called each living creature, that was its name* (Genesis 2:19 NIV).

And then God later made woman for the purpose of being a helper to the man. *The Lord God said, "It is not good for the man to be alone. I will make a helper suitable for him"* (Genesis 2:18 NIV).

God gave man and his helper (woman), a great job to do together. He had a purpose for their lives. He told them to be His appointed guardians over His creation and to rule over all things. *God blessed them and said to them, "Be fruitful and increase in number; fill the earth and subdue it. Rule over the fish in the sea and the birds in the sky and over every living creature that moves on the ground"* (Genesis 1:28 NIV).

After man disobeyed God and sinned, the conditions surrounding the work environment changed. Work became a struggle filled with many obstacles that pushed the man and woman to their physical limits.

"Cursed is the ground because of you; through painful toil you will eat food from it all the days of your life. It will produce thorns and thistles for you, and you will eat the plants of the field. By the sweat of your brow you will eat your food until you return to the ground, since from it you were taken; for dust you are and to dust you will return" (Genesis 3:17-18 NIV).

The woman's life also changed. She was placed under the man's authority and required to endure terrible pain during childbirth. *To the woman he said, "I will make your pains in childbearing very severe; with painful labor you will give birth to children. Your desire will be for your husband, and he will rule over you"* (Genesis 3:16 NIV).

God has always intended for man to work. But after man sinned, the work experience and the conditions surrounding the work environment changed greatly. Work is not easy, but it is necessary. It often pushes us to our limits. *Anyone who does not provide for their relatives, and especially for their own household, has denied the faith and is worse than an unbeliever* (1 Timothy 5:8 NIV).

Work Attitude

The attitude in which you approach your work is the key element that God is concerned about. A Christian with the right attitude carries a tremendous testimony for God in the work place. As Christians, our attitude at work should reflect the heart of a servant. Charles Spurgeon once said, *"There are no crown-wearers in Heaven who were not cross-bearers below."*

In order to lead, you must first learn how to serve. God has a purpose for every person based on how He shaped that person.

You shaped me first inside, then out; you formed me in my mother's womb... You know me inside and out, you know every bone in my body; You know exactly how I was made, bit by bit... Like an open book, you watched me grow from conception to birth; All the stages of my life were spread out before you, the days of my life all prepared before I'd even lived one day! (Psalm 139:13 MSG).

No matter what you do in life to provide for yourself and your family, God wants you to do it with the right attitude, as though He was evaluating you.

And whatever you do, whether in word or deed, do it all in the name of the Lord Jesus, giving thanks to God the Father through him. Whatever you do, work at it with all your heart, as working for the Lord, not for human masters, since you know that you will receive an inheritance from the Lord as a reward. It is the Lord Christ you are serving (Colossians 3:17, 23, 24 NIV).

There are many jobs you can do, but God has shaped you for a certain type of work. He wants you to work hard and to become the best you can be in a job that is suited for the way you are shaped. In doing so, you will please God.

Observe people who are good at their work—skilled workers are always in demand and admired; they don't take a backseat to anyone (Proverbs 22:29 MSG).

Whatever your hand finds to do, do it with all your might (Ecclesiastes 9:10 NIV).

Work Ethic

A poor work ethic is evident when a worker is more concerned with what they gain rather than what they contribute—workers who are trying to get as much as they can while giving the least that they must. *One who is slack in his work is brother to one who destroys* (Proverbs 18:9 NIV).

A poor work ethic encourages a lazy, slothful attitude is very contagious and can ruin a good testimony. *Lazy hands make for poverty, but diligent hands bring wealth* (Proverbs 10:4 NIV).

Diligent hands will rule, but laziness ends in forced labor (Proverbs 12:24 NIV).

Scripture warns that the lazy worker will always be hungry. *A sluggard's appetite is never filled, but the desires of the diligent are fully satisfied* (Proverbs 13:4). God expects you to work when you are physically and mentally able to do so.

The following passage gives a great visual example of what happens to a person who is lazy and hates to work.

One day I walked by the field of an old lazybones, and then passed the vineyard of a lout; They were overgrown with weeds, thick with thistles, all the fences broken down. I took a long look and pondered what I saw; the fields preached me a sermon and I listened: "A nap here, a nap there, a day off here, a day off there, sit back, take it easy—do you know what comes next? Just this: You can look forward to a dirt-poor life, with poverty as your permanent houseguest!" (Proverbs 24:30-34 MSG).

Paul stated it best when he said: *For even when we were with you, we gave you this rule: "The one who is unwilling to work shall not eat." We hear that some among you are idle and disruptive. They are not busy; they are busybodies* (2 Thessalonians 3:10-11 NIV).

Work does more for you than simply providing you with a wage. Work is necessary for your well being on many levels. When you are a productive part of society, you develop a sense of self worth. An honest day of work is a way for you to give back to society and find value in your life.

Time is Your Most Valuable Asset

Our fast-paced world often destroys the balance that is so important to the Christian's life. Balancing time with God, family, work, church, recreation, etc. is constantly strained. An Amish man once said, "*The hurrier I go, the behinder I get!*" Oh, how true.

All the stuff in life you think is so important often robs you of your valuable time. You think about it, research it, talk to friends about it, shop for it, and eventually buy it. Then you must care for it until it breaks, is worn out, or you eventually get tired of it or feel the need to replace it with the newer, more improved model. Then the cycle starts all over again. Not only does the process stress you to an unhealthy level, your urgency in the pursuit of materialism blinds you to God's wisdom and purpose for your life.

In *The Paradox of Time*, Henry Dobson said, "Time goes," you say. "Ah, no! Alas, time stays! You go!" Becoming an excellent manager of your *life* requires you to be a disciplined manager of your *time*. Time is your most valuable asset and needs to receive your urgent attention.

Work Quality

Your attitude toward work and money can be easily distorted unless filtered through the sound wisdom and principles found in God's Word. One such principle tells us that we need to be honest and consistent in our work and avoid desiring to find shortcuts that often take advantage of others. *Dishonest money dwindles away, but whoever gathers money little by little makes it grow* (Proverbs 13:11 NIV).

Those who work their land will have abundant food, but those who chase fantasies will have their fill of poverty (Proverbs 28:19 NIV).

It takes time to plan and build a good business and to provide a quality product or service for your customers. *The plans of the diligent lead to profit as surely as haste leads to poverty* (Proverbs 21:5 NIV).

People quickly recognize quality and excellence and are eager to tell others. This is a foundational principle in God's Word. *God's plan for building wealth is one of orderliness and excellence in His time, not haste.* Proverbs 21:5 (NIV)

Regardless if you own your own business or are employed by someone else, the sound principles in God's Word always work. It is to your advantage to understand them and apply them in your dealings with your work and money. Here are a few more verses to meditate on:

All hard work brings a profit, but mere talk leads only to poverty (Proverbs 14:23 NIV).

A faithful person will be richly blessed, but one eager to get rich will not go unpunished. Proverbs 28:20 (NIV)

The stingy are eager to get rich and are unaware that poverty awaits them (Proverbs 28:22 NIV).

Quite often, young couples are eager to buy their first house as soon as possible. Wisdom from God's Word teaches that before you commit yourself to buying a house, you should first establish your income: *Do your planning and prepare your fields before building your house* (Proverbs 24:27 NIV).

This might mean renting until you have saved an adequate down payment and your income is sufficient to support a mortgage. I had to learn this lesson the hard way when I bought my first house too early and too big.

A wrong attitude will almost always create an emotional trap that will result in unwise financial decisions. Fueled by wants and desires, you can easily become overextended with a house you can't afford to furnish or maintain. A wrong attitude makes it easy for you to be tempted to finance new automobiles and enjoy entertainment and shopping without restraint. Before you realize it, you and your spouse are arguing about spending decisions that otherwise would have not been an issue. Decisions made as a result of wrong attitudes begins a pattern for making more wrong decisions. Instead of financial freedom, you will find yourself in financial bondage.

It would be wise to always seek the counsel of those you respect before making large financial commitments. Next, you should take the matter to God and spend time in His Word and prayer. If you are married, you should pray about it together.

If you are not careful, with the encouragement and approval of the world, your obsession with materialism will become a way of life. You might even justify your behavior with the thought: *Everyone is doing it.* Well, just because everybody else is doing it doesn't make it right…matter of fact, if everyone else is doing it, it is probably wrong. *The way of fools seems right to them, but the wise listen to advice* (Proverbs 12:15 NIV).

Very few people are living their lives in accordance with God's principles. *There's a way of life that looks harmless enough; look again—it leads straight to hell. Sure, those people appear to be having a good time, but all that laughter will end in heartbreak* (Proverbs 14:12-13 MSG).

Parable of the Two Builders

One last parable that points to the importance of "doing" God's wisdom in your life is the *Parable of the Two Builders*. In this parable, Jesus illustrates the importance of application.

"These words I speak to you are not incidental additions to your life, homeowner improvements to your standard of living. They are foundational words, words to build a life on. If you work these words into your life, you are like a smart carpenter who built his house on solid rock. Rain poured down, the river flooded, a tornado hit—but nothing moved that house. It was

fixed to the rock.

"But if you just use my words in Bible studies and don't work them into your life, you are like a stupid carpenter who built his house on the sandy beach. When a storm rolled in and the waves came up, it collapsed like a house of cards" (Matthew 7:24-27 MSG).

Do your work to the glory of God rather than for the approval of man. Be diligent in all you do and a disciplined manager of your time. Let your work reflect an attitude of service, responsibility, and quality beyond what your customers or your employers expect.

God gives you a great opportunity to be a living testimony to Him in your work. *Do you see any truly competent workers? They will serve kings rather than working for ordinary people* (Proverbs 22:29 NLT).

PART TWO
Application

Chapter Four
The Importance of Planning

The Small Business Administration once said that the number one reason small businesses fail is poor planning. The home is nothing more than a small business that God has appointed you to manage. The finances of every Christian home should be a testimony of orderliness and excellence to a world driven by greed, envy, and indulgence.

Does the Bible teach that a family should have a financial plan? In a marriage, who is responsible for developing a financial plan? What are the benefits of having a financial plan?

Planning is critical if you hope to have an orderly life. From a Christian perspective, we are much like the manager of a small business. We don't own it, we manage it for God. *We plan the way we want to live, but only God makes us able to live it* (Proverbs 16:9 MSG).

A budget outlines a plan for spending, saving, and giving. It doesn't have to be fancy, but every family needs a written plan (budget). If you are married, you and your spouse must agree on the plan. As managers (stewards), you are negligent with God's money when you refuse to develop and follow a plan for your home. Just like with a small business, it is impossible for you to efficiently manage your finances without a written plan. As you plan, you must be flexible and sensitive to God's leading as He orchestrates the divine circumstances in your life.

Bottom line: It is all about being a prudent manager of God's resources so that your purposes become His purposes. *We humans keep brainstorming options and plans, but God's purpose prevails* (Proverbs 19:21 MSG).

Prerequisites to Planning

Before you begin putting your plan on paper, you should first review your needs and goals and commit them to God.

Commit to the Lord whatever you do, and he will establish your plans (Proverbs 16:3 NIV).

The amount of money you have to work with is not important. It is about what you do with what you have, as Jesus emphasized in the *Parable of the Talents*. God is also looking at your relationship with money. Does your love of money cause you to lose your focus and compromise your testimony? *Better a little with righteousness than much gain with injustice* (Proverbs 16:8 NIV).

You must also be extremely cautious of pride—especially if God has decided to give you a relatively large amount to manage. Pride is a very dangerous sin that has the potential of destroying your reputation, your business, and your life. *The Lord detests all the proud of heart. Be sure of this: They will not go unpunished* (Proverbs 16:5 NIV).

First pride, then the crash—the bigger the ego, the harder the fall (Proverbs 16:18 MSG).

When your plans are established with God's stamp of approval, you can be assured that it has been done right. *When God approves of your life, even your enemies will end up shaking your hand* (Proverbs 16:7 MSG).

The way you plan to spend the money that God has given you to manage will be a direct reflection of the convictions in your heart. And finally, if you are unsure what to do or how to do it, pray and ask God. *If any of you lacks wisdom, you should ask God, who gives generously to all without finding fault, and it will be given to you* (James 1:5 NIV).

Planning: The Responsibility of a Leader

Newly married couples beginning their lives together are under tremendous pressure. They want it all: the new cars; the new house; the fancy toys. With entry-level incomes and minimal savings, they often turn to easy credit. They assume that their incomes will increase before their debts consume them. This dangerous attitude is responsible for destroying many good marriages. Jesus offers us some wise advice in the *Parable of the Two Builders.*

"Is there anyone here who, planning to build a new house, doesn't first sit down and figure the cost so you'll know if you can complete it? If you only get the foundation laid and then run out of money, you're going to look pretty foolish. Everyone passing by will poke fun at you: 'He started something he couldn't finish'" (Luke 14:28-30 MSG).

A written spending plan for the family (budget), allows you to carefully consider and track the "goings" of your money. Without a written plan, you become a responder—one who reacts rather than controls. If you don't control the spending process, you will one day wake up to find that there is more month than money, or worse, more life than money. *Be sure you know the condition of your flocks, give careful attention to your herds; for riches do not endure forever, and a crown is not secure for all generations* (Proverbs 27:23, 24 NIV).

In every Christian home, God has appointed a leader. Except in the case of singles, that person is the husband and father. The leader of a Christian home has the God-given position of responsibility to provide for that home. *Anyone who does not provide for their relatives, and especially for their own household, has denied the faith and is worse than an unbeliever* (1 Timothy 5:8 NIV).

The leader of a home must be prudent in his dealings with money. He is ultimately responsible even though he might seek advice from others—including professionals. *The gullible believe anything they're told; the prudent sift and weigh every word* (Proverbs 14:15 MSG).

It is his responsibility to understand budgeting, investing, financing, mortgages, insurance, and debt. Webster's Dictionary defines "prudent" as, "exercising sound judgment in practical matters, cautious in conduct; managing carefully."

Although the leader is ultimately responsible to God, it is vitally important that the development of the budget plan be made collectively by everyone who has a part in making the plan work.

Without a written plan, the outcome of your months, years, or even your entire life, is at best only a guess. Budget plans must be flexible and visible. If you are the leader of your home, God has made you responsible for your finances. However, it cannot be over emphasized that those involved in executing the plan should have an active part in its design.

The Results of a Wise Plan

The story of Jacob's youngest son, Joseph, teaches us an excellent lesson about the importance of planning (Genesis chapters 37–47).

Joseph's older brothers were jealous and hated him because their father favored the younger Joseph. When Joseph was only seventeen years old, his brothers trapped him and sold as a slave. Joseph endured many more trials and temptations, but because he remained strong in his faith, the Lord blessed Joseph.

God had a great purpose for Joseph's life. His close relationship with the Lord allowed him to be able to interpret the dream of the Pharaoh of Egypt. After his interpretation of the dream, he presented a master plan to Pharaoh that was responsible for saving all of Egypt from starvation.

The first thing Joseph did was set aside 20% reserves during the good years to be used during the bad years.

Let Pharaoh appoint commissioners over the land to take a fifth of the harvest of Egypt during the seven years of abundance. They should collect all the food of these good years that are coming and store up the grain under the authority of Pharaoh, to be kept in the cities for food. This food should be held in reserve for the country, to be used during the seven years of famine that will come upon Egypt, so that the country may not be ruined by the famine (Genesis 41:34-36 NIV).

The Pharaoh liked Joseph's plan. *The plan seemed good to*

Pharaoh and to all his officials (Genesis 41:37 NIV).

He also recognized that God's wisdom was responsible for Joseph's plan. *Then Pharaoh said to Joseph, "Since God has made all this known to you, there is no one so discerning and wise as you* (Genesis 41:39 NIV).

Pharaoh was so pleased that he elevated Joseph to the second highest position in Egypt. *You shall be in charge of my palace, and all my people are to submit to your orders. Only with respect to the throne will I be greater than you* (Genesis 41:40 NIV).

When you obey God and live by His principles, you are promised blessings. This is seen in the story of Joseph's life. Whether on a national scale or a personal scale, God's wisdom never fails. As was seen with Joseph, planning is critical if you are to maximize the resources God has entrusted to you. Only by proving yourself to be worthy will God find use for you in His service. It is in service for God that you find His blessings. *God's blessing makes life rich; nothing we do can improve on God* (Proverbs 10:22 MSG).

Chapter Five
Living without Debt

Does the Bible teach that it is wrong to borrow money? What does surety mean? Is it wrong for a Christian to finance an automobile?

Debt is the most common way that people get themselves and their families into financial bondage. Believe it or not, living without debt is possible—even today in our consumption-based economy.

You must start to think differently from the secular society and develop a debt-free mind set. *Do not conform any longer to the pattern of this world, but be transformed by the renewing of your mind* (Romans 12:2a NIV).

To Borrow or Not to Borrow

Does the Bible say that it is wrong to borrow money? No. The Bible does not prohibit the Christian from borrowing. However, it does teach that it would be better if you didn't. God wants to bless you. He can only bless you if you are willing to diligently follow his advice. He ultimately wants you to be in a position to help others. When you borrow, you forfeit a piece of your freedom: *Just as the rich rule the poor, so the borrower is servant to the lender* (Proverbs 22:7 NLT).

The following passage of scripture from Deuteronomy very clearly addresses the blessing and the curse of God. Pay particular attention to the references to borrowing and lending. God's blessing and His curse are real things and have real effects. The blessing of God's favor is promised to those who diligently listen to and obey His voice. When God blesses you, you will be given the opportunity to become a blessing to others.

God will lavish you with good things: children from your womb, offspring from your animals, and crops from your land, the land that God promised your ancestors that he would give you.

God will throw open the doors of his sky vaults and pour rain on your land on schedule and bless the work you take in hand. You will lend to many nations but you yourself won't have to take out a loan.

God will make you the head, not the tail; you'll always be the top dog, never the bottom dog, as you obediently listen to and diligently keep the commands of God your God, that I am commanding you today.

Don't swerve an inch to the right or left from the words that I command you today by going off following and worshiping other gods (Deuteronomy 28: 11-14 MSG).

When you are a responsible and obedient manager of what God has entrusted to you, you put yourself in a position to be used to help others by giving and lending. *Give to the one who asks you, and do not turn away from the one who wants to borrow from you* (Matthew 5:42 NIV).

Jesus went a step further in clarification of God's idea of making a loan. He suggested that any loans you make be made without expecting repayment or interest.

Here is a simple rule of thumb for behavior: Ask yourself what you want people to do for you; then grab the initiative and do it for them! If you only love the lovable, do you expect a pat on the back? Run-of-the-mill sinners do that. If you only help those who help you, do you expect a medal? Garden-variety sinners do that. If you only give for what you hope to get out of it, do you think that's charity? The stingiest of pawnbrokers does that (Luke 6:31-34 MSG).

As a manager of God's resources, you must be extremely sensitive to what He wants you to do with what He has given you to manage. It is not your responsibility to meet the never ending needs of the irresponsible, but when you walk closely with God, you will know who, when, and how much to help those that are truly in need. He will not ask you to help someone unless He has provided you the means to do it. There is also a danger of becoming an enabler and helping someone financially when God is using their need to draw them closer to Him. The only way to be an effective manager of God's resources is to be still and listen to His voice within. You will be blessed when you do as He instructs.

Do not withhold good from those to whom it is due, when it is in your power to act. Do not say to your neighbor, "Come back tomorrow and I'll give it to you"—when you already have it with you (Proverbs 3:27-28 NIV).

Two Rules to Remember if You Plan to Borrow

RULE #1: If you borrow, remember that it is your responsibility to repay what you owe in full.

It is better not to make a vow than to make one and not fulfill it (Ecclesiastes 5:5 NIV).

The wicked borrow and do not repay, but the righteous give generously; (Psalm 37:21 NIV).

During difficult times, it becomes a true test of your trust in God to do what is right. In an effort to guard your assets, there is sometimes the temptation to withhold from paying debts. Because of a sinful attitude, Chapter 13 bankruptcies have become a very popular and socially accepted way to be forgiven of large amounts of unsecured debt. The sole purpose for a bankruptcy should be to provide you more time to repay your creditors, not simply to allow you to be forgiven of the debts.

A sterling reputation is better than striking it rich; a gracious spirit is better than money in the bank (Proverbs 22:1 MSG).

Simply put, when you borrow, you must repay. It is a sin for you to think otherwise, even in times of hardship. You must remember, if you choose to borrow, God requires you to repay it in full. It is our moral and spiritual responsibility. When Paul was talking about our responsibility to pay taxes, he highlighted a very important principle.

Let no debt remain outstanding, except the continuing debt to love one another, for whoever loves others has fulfilled the law (Romans 13:8 NIV).

RULE #2: Never become surety for a debt. Webster's Dictionary defines surety as; *something that gives assurance, as against loss*; *one who makes himself responsible for another*.

Surety results when you agree to cosign for someone who is borrowing money. The definition of "someone" could be a family member, a friend, a business partner, a bank, or a mortgage company, to name a few.

My son, if you have put up security for your neighbor, if you have shaken hands in pledge for a stranger, you have been trapped by what you said, ensnared by the words of your mouth (Proverbs 6:1-2 NIV).

One example of surety might be a parent cosigning with a child to finance an automobile. If for any reason the child is unable or unwilling to make the payments on the loan, the parent becomes solely responsible for the debt—even if the parent does not have access to the automobile.

Surety can occur with any automobile loan. Let's assume that after three years you owe $8,000 on a car loan, but the value of the car is only $4,000. If you only have $1,000 available in cash, you would be surety for the loan to the amount of $3,000. The only way to avoid surety is if you have an absolute certain way to repay the loan; in this example you don't.

Another example would be cosigning with a partner in a service-related business. If the business fails and there are not enough assets to collateralize the loan, you and your partner become personally responsible for the debt. If your partner is unable to pay his portion of the debt, you become liable for the entire debt.

Whoever puts up security for a stranger will surely suffer, but whoever refuses to shake hands in pledge is safe (Proverbs 11:15 NIV).

Taking this a step closer to home, when you sign an agreement with a bank for a credit card, you become partners with that bank. If you are planning to use the credit card for financing consumer goods and services (clothes, food, gasoline, furniture, vacations, etc.), you are subjecting yourself to potential surety.

For example, let's assume you had a credit limit of $5,000 on your credit card, but only $1,000 in cash. At anytime your credit card balance exceeds $1,000, you become surety for your debts.

You might assume that, just because you have income from your job to service the debts, everything is fine. If this is your rational, you are in effect cosigning with your employer for the balance of your debt.

What happens if you lose your job? It would be as if your partner (your employer) is releasing themselves from the obligation to help you continue to service your debt. The first mistake you made was assuming. It is not prudent to assume things will work out.

The prudent see danger and take refuge, but the simple keep going and pay the penalty (Proverbs 22:3 NIV).

When you become surety for a debt, or for the debt of another, you are personally taking responsibility to pay the debt without the collateral to back it. Becoming surety for a debt is a violation of Biblical principles.

Do not be one who shakes hands in pledge or puts up security for debts (Proverbs 22:26 NIV).

One who has no sense shakes hands in pledge and puts up security for a neighbor (Proverbs 17:18 NIV).

God is as much concerned about the relationships you have with your family, friends, partners, and lenders as He is with you maintaining a life that is free from worry, fear, stress, and anxiety. His principles are for your protection and aimed to help you stay in a position of thankfulness to Him.

When you are in a right relationship with God, you are best able to fulfill the purpose He has designed for your life. When you live according to His plan and purpose for your life, you will be in the best possible position to love and serve others.

The Dangers of Debt

Thomas Jefferson once said, "*I place economy among the first and most important virtues, and public debt as the greatest dangers.*"

71

God warns: *The poor are always ruled over by the rich, so don't borrow and put yourself under their power* (Proverbs 22:7 MSG).

Western society has become comfortable with using easy credit as an alternative means of satisfying their obsession for stuff. Easy credit in the hands of an undisciplined and ignorant consumer is a recipe for disaster.

From 1930 to 1940, debt was virtually nonexistent. From 1950 to 1960, banks began to loan money for the purchase of homes. From 1960 to 1970, financing automobiles became commonplace. During the '70s, '80s, and '90, the use of credit was made available for almost anything. Credit card debt exploded!

I remember the first month I turned sixteen (November 1970) and got my driver's license. Excited to enjoy my independence, I would often pick up a friend after school, or some Saturday afternoon, and we would go "cruising". Cruising was defined as driving around town with no specific destination in mind. My parents had graciously given me a Shell credit card to use for gas. On a good Saturday of cruising, I might fill the gas tank two times. Life couldn't have been better. Needless to say, I quickly lost the privilege of a gas card when my dad opened his December Shell statement.

Easy credit makes it difficult for the Christian to trust God. Instead of waiting for God to supply the means, the Christian often acts on impulse and borrows the money without a second thought. Instead of praying about every purchase, emotions entice the person to follow the secular world down the path to destruction. Pride and greed cry out for the new car, the stylish clothes, and the larger house—often too large for the family budget.

Pride goes before destruction, a haughty spirit before a fall (Proverbs 16:18 NIV).

The Christian who chooses to live apart from the wisdom of God's Word will reap the consequences of their foolishness. The results of becoming surety, defaulting on loans, and other unwise and sinful practices regarding finances brings suffering into the home.

The road to financial destruction is littered with damaged relationships and broken marriages. The children in these families repeat the foolish behavior of their parents. They do so because of their lack of wise mentors and examples of Godly character and obedience. Generations will suffer when the sound principles in God's Word are ignored.

The less you are entangled in the world's ways, the more available you will be to God. *Therefore, since we are surrounded by such a great cloud of witnesses, let us throw off everything that hinders and the sin that so easily entangles* (Hebrews 12:1(a) NIV).

Becoming a Wise Saver

An important part of a wise budget plan is savings. After you have developed a reasonable plan for spending and giving, you need to allocate part of your income to savings. The story of Joseph, in the previous chapter, is a great example of the importance of developing a plan for saving. Joseph saved 25% during the good years to prepare for the bad years. His disciplined plan provided for the entire nation—including his brothers who had betrayed him.

God warns that, within your ability, it is your responsibility to provide for your family. *Anyone who does not provide for their relatives, and especially for their own household, has denied the faith and is worse than an unbeliever* (1 Timothy 5:8 NIV).

Because the future is unknown, there will always be unexpected financial requirements, but it is your responsibility to be a wise and prudent planner. A wise plan will include a reasonable amount of funds set aside to provide for unscheduled expenses.

Now listen, you who say, "Today or tomorrow we will go to this or that city, spend a year there, carry on business and make money." Why, you do not even know what will happen tomorrow. What is your life? You are a mist that appears for a little while and then vanishes (James 4:13-14 NIV).

Savings put aside for emergencies maintains flexibility in your budget. Tomorrow is filled with uncertainty, but a wise man is prepared for the unknown. *The wise store up choice food and olive oil, but fools gulp theirs down* (Proverbs 21:20 NIV).

The wise man has a plan. The fool lives for today. *A prudent person sees trouble coming and ducks; a simpleton walks in blindly and is clobbered* (Proverbs 27:12 MSG).

You must expect life to be filled with trouble and unexpected events and occurrences. When you choose to disregard this known fact, you can expect to get clobbered.

Giving God His Place

Before you call upon the secular world to supply your needs, go to God. As you learn to transfer more and more of your trust to Him, you will see His faithfulness as He promised. When you borrow from the world, you are volunteering to enter into a servant relationship with those who do not follow God. Take your needs to the Lord first, then to your church. Typically, when there is a need, someone else has an abundance who is asking God how it is to be used.

Give God the opportunity to make your life a testimony by trusting Him for everything. *Call on me in the day of trouble; I will deliver you, and you will honor me* (Psalm 50:15 NIV).

Do not be anxious about anything, but in every situation, by prayer and petition, with thanksgiving, present your requests to God. And my God will meet all your needs according to the riches of his glory in Christ Jesus (Philippians 4:6, 19 NIV).

Be afraid of debt. Respect it and avoid it when possible. Debt robs more people of their freedom than anything else. In most cases, debt is not necessary. Debt is usually a voluntary act of imprisonment. Yes, you can live without debt!

76

Formula for Getting Out of D-E-B-T

D-iscipline in your actions

E-xcellence in your attitude

B-udget all your resources

T-ime will pay your debt

Chapter Six
Releasing the Blessing

What does the Bible teach about sowing and reaping? What is the difference between giving a tithe, giving an offering, and giving sacrificially? When is it wrong to give?

The book of Philippians ends with the greatest promise in the Bible: *You can be sure that God will take care of everything you need, His generosity exceeding yours, in the glory that pours from Jesus* (Philippians 4:19 MSG).

The Philippians understood what it meant to be financially free. The church at Philippi was famous for their generosity. Paul's letter to the Philippians was a thank you note to them for their extreme generosity. Paul even used the Philippians' generosity as an example when he wrote to other churches.

Speaking of the Philippians, Paul said in Corinthians: *In the midst of a very severe trial, their overflowing joy and their extreme poverty welled up in rich generosity...they gave as much as they were able, and even beyond their ability... they exceeded our expectations: They gave themselves first of all to the Lord, and then by the will of God also to us* (2 Corinthians 8:2-5 NIV).

When Paul stated the promise to the Philippians: *...God will take care of everything you need...* he meant *everything*. Paul knew that with every promise there is a prerequisite. In the case of the Philippians, they had satisfied the prerequisites of being assured that God would take care of their every need. Paul stated that God's generosity would exceed theirs.

The law of sowing and reaping is a universal law: *Whoever sows sparingly will also reap sparingly, and whoever sows generously will also reap generously* (2 Corinthians 9:6 NIV).

If you plant a corn seed, you get a stalk of corn with one or two ears of corn. If you plant a bean, you get multiple beans. What you give, you get back—usually in an amount larger than you gave. If you want a friend, be a friend to someone else. If you need more time, give some of your time to helping people. The principle of sowing and reaping applies in every area of life. *The merciful, kind, and generous man benefits himself* (Proverbs 11:17 AMP).

When Jesus was asked which was the greatest commandment in the Law, *Jesus replied: "Love the Lord your God with all your heart and with all your soul and with all your mind." This is the first and greatest commandment. And the second is like it: "Love your neighbor as yourself"* (Matthew 22:37-39 NIV).

To live a life of generosity in a state of being that is completely free from the cares of the world, you must maintain an eternal perspective. This is done by staying focused on the Cross of Christ. The Cross might seem to be a small thing, but from the Biblical perspective it is of more importance than all the empires of the world. The Cross is where the Christian obtains spiritual strength. When you lose your spiritual strength, you stop relying on God and stop living by God's priorities and principles. In essence, you stop loving Him.

As Jesus stated, God wants us to love Him before anything else. Secondly, he wants us to love and serve others. If you are completely honest with yourself, you will most likely agree that the default setting for humans is to serve self first, others second, and turn to God only when there is a need. To be truly free, you must reverse the order and put God first, others second, and yourself last. This is especially true when it comes to your relationship with money. Don't wait for God to bring you to a sudden stop before you change or remove the attitude that stands between you and Him.

Money (or something of value that can be bartered) is the common thread that has connected people since the beginning of time. We exchange it for the goods and services necessary to live. But when money is believed to have the power to satisfy your deepest desires, obtaining more of it will become your greatest love. Freedom from the love of money occurs when you embrace the Biblical truth that "God owns it all and everything you have is a gift from Him."

Job acknowledged the truth of God's ownership when he said: *"When I was born into this world, I was naked and had nothing. When I die and leave this world, I will be naked and have nothing. The Lord gives, and the Lord takes away. Praise the name of the Lord!"* (Job 1:21 ERV).

Freedom is not determined by what you have, it is determined by what you surrender. When you give, you will get back. When you give up control, you get freedom. True freedom becomes a reality when you claim ownership to nothing and entrust everything—your health, your job, your family, your material possessions—to God. Everything you are given, including your life, is meant to be used for God's glory.

If you start thinking to yourselves, "I did all this. And all by myself. I'm rich. It's all mine!"—well, think again. Remember that God, your God, gave you the strength to produce all this wealth so as to confirm the covenant that he promised to your ancestors—as it is today (Deuteronomy 8:17-18 MSG).

Once I accepted my rightful place as a manager instead of an owner, I was instantly and completely freed from money's grip on my life. It is something I must continue to work on. My state of freedom is dependent on my state of surrender to God's design. Only then will I be blessed by God and be able to be a blessing to others.

Scripture teaches that giving is a direct pipeline to blessings. So buckle up and let's talk about being a blessing by giving *it* away. I promise it won't be nearly as painful if you stay focused on the fact that it is not yours in the first place. After all, from where God sits, you own nothing!

What you give away brings you a greater blessing than what you receive. Jesus said, *It is more blessed to give than to receive* (Acts 20:35 NIV). That should be enough to make us line up to give. Do you believe it? Do you want to be blessed? Then give.

The promises of blessing and generosity from God should make us cheerfully generous. *Give, and it will be given to you. A good measure, pressed down, shaken together and running over, will be poured into your lap. For with the measure you use, it will be measured to you* (Luke 6:38 NIV). It's a question of faith. It's a question of trust. It's a question of belief. You either believe it or you don't.

There are two conditions that allow a person to be a cheerful giver: 1) when the money belongs to someone else; 2) when there is no suffering as a result of giving it away. For the Christian who has accepted his/her position as a manager, as opposed to an owner, both of these conditions are met. The Bible teaches that *everything* you have belongs to God, and, if you live according to God's principles, His blessings will provide provision for your needs. So, with the right attitude, every Christian can be a cheerful giver.

Each of you should give what you have decided in your heart to give, not reluctantly or under compulsion, for God loves a cheerful giver (2 Corinthians 9:7 NIV).

When NOT To Give

If you ever feel pressured to give, don't. You don't get any credit for that kind of gift. God's not looking at the amount you give but at your attitude.

Giving always has been, and always will be, an *opportunity* for the Christian. God does not punish you when you do not give—you simply forfeit His blessings. Jesus said, *Whoever sows sparingly will also reap sparingly, and whoever sows generously will also reap generously* (2 Corinthians 9:6 NIV).

The Christian must also understand that giving is not a step towards personal surrender to God; it is something you do as a result of having *already* surrendered to Him. When you focus on the giving, you miss the purpose God intended. Opportunities to give are opportunities God is giving you to be blessed. He can just as easily bypass you and let someone else get the blessing. Receiving God's blessings are a result of your attitude more than a result of what you give. God doesn't want or need your money; what He wants is all of you.

As you become faithful managers of what God has placed in your care, you will learn to be sensitive to the leading of the Holy Spirit in the wise use of all of the resources He places in your care—money, time, talents, etc. With each step of faith, God will reveal more and more of Himself to you. With each step of faith, you gain a new attitude, a new strength, a new testimony, and a new freedom.

Getting control of your financial life allows you to respond more freely to God as He touches your heart in different opportunities of service and giving. When you live an orderly and excellent life as a wise and faithful manager, you have the opportunity to become a tremendous asset to the ministry of God through your local church and through your personal testimony.

For example, living on a budget plan allows you to identify true surpluses that God directs into your life. Being sensitive to His leading, you can then direct those surpluses to the areas He has planned.

At the present time your plenty will supply what they need, so that in turn their plenty will supply what you need (2 Corinthians 8:14 NIV).

Without a plan for your finances, you can be assured that you will never be able to identify a surplus.

If God chooses to give you an abundance (surplus), you incur a great responsibility to seek His guidance as to its use.

From everyone who has been given much, much will be demanded; and from the one who has been entrusted with much, much more will be asked (Luke 12:48(b) NIV).

Blessed with an abundance doesn't automatically mean that you should give to every person that approaches you with a need. It is not always a bad thing when someone is experiencing a tough time financially. God uses many circumstances to draw us closer to Him. Money is a great tool to get someone's attention. God often uses a financial shortfall to encourage obedience, faithfulness, and trust. Therefore, only as God burdens your heart should you offer to meet someone's need.

Each of you should give what you have decided in your heart to give, not reluctantly or under compulsion, for God loves a cheerful giver. And God is able to bless you abundantly, so that in all things at all times, having all that you need, you will abound in every good work (2 Corinthians 9:7-8 NIV).

Needless to say, you can only hear God when you are ready and prepared to listen. You must *desire* His will not yours. You must be surrendered.

Whoever belongs to God hears what God says. The reason you do not hear is that you do not belong to God (John 8:47 NIV).

Three Ways to Give

There are basically three ways to give a portion of the money God has entrusted to you: First, a tenth (tithe); second, an offering from a surplus; and third, through sacrifice.

The Tithe

Regular giving presents the opportunity for Christians to give a material testimony to the fact that God is Sovereign, King, Owner, and Lord! In addition, giving the tithe is a good starting place. Giving on a regular basis is a physical reminder that you do not own anything. God owns it all!

When you view regular giving as a duty or a rule, it becomes legalism. The Bible makes clear that when the gift is "given" as a result of legalism, it is in vain and will not return God's blessings. If you give an offering for the purpose of receiving God's blessings; this too is wrong. Your gifts should be offered solely as a result of having the proper perspective that God is the Owner and Giver of all things. Your gifts should be the result of your love, respect, and fear of God.

The things God places in your care are for the purpose of serving Him. When you claim ownership to these things, you rob God. Your regular gifts are nothing more than the first step in the acknowledgment that God is truly the Owner of it all!

Honor God with everything you own; give him the first and the best (Proverbs 3:9 MSG).

Old Testament history tells us that the "Law" required that all Jews make offerings that exceeded 20% annually, but it should be pointed out that the "Law" had no influence on the decision that these men made to give a material testimony to God. The tithe was only a minimum of what God asked of them in order for them to see His blessings.

Bring the full amount of your tithes to the Temple, so that there will be plenty of food there. Put me to the test and you will see that I will open the windows of heaven and pour out on you in abundance all kinds of good things (Malachi 3:10 GNT).

The prophet Malachi directed his message of judgment to a people who had become so sinful as a nation that God's words no longer had any impact in their lives.

I ask you, is it right for a person to cheat God? Of course not, yet you are cheating me. 'How?' you ask. In the matter of tithes and offerings. A curse is on all of you because the whole nation is cheating me (Malachi 3:8-9 GNT).

In order to believe that your regular gifts are an important step of faith, there must be an alignment of your attitude with the teachings of the Bible. Your faith must be followed by your faithfulness. When this happens, you will begin to experience the blessings of the Lord. The principle of giving, as a result of the right attitude, is the key that opens the door to God's blessings in the life of the Christian.

In the following verses, Jesus rebuked the Pharisees. Even though they tithed, their attitude was wrong.

"Woe to you, teachers of the law and Pharisees, you

hypocrites! You give a tenth of your spices—mint, dill and cumin. But you have neglected the more important matters of the law—justice, mercy and faithfulness.*

"You should have practiced the latter, without neglecting the former. You blind guides! You strain out a gnat but swallow a camel. Woe to you, teachers of the law and Pharisees, you hypocrites! You clean the outside of the cup and dish, but inside they are full of greed and self-indulgence" (Matthew 23:23-25 NIV).

Paul makes it clear to the Macedonians what they should give to the Lord first—before they gave their money. *Each of you should give what you have decided in your heart to give, not reluctantly or under compulsion, for God loves a cheerful giver.* (2 Corinthians 9:7 NIV).

Every Christian should give proportionally from what God has given them. It should be a regular gift from the first and best fruits of their labors.

Honor the Lord by making him an offering from the best of all that your land produces (Proverbs 3:9 GNT).

It should be given as a result of your love for God and your desire to obey Him and surrender completely to His will for your life. But first, give your entire self to Him. *And they exceeded our expectations: They gave themselves first of all to the Lord, and then by the will of God also to us* (2 Corinthians 8:5 NIV).

The Surplus

Giving from surplus is truly a blessing from the Lord. This money is given as an offering above and beyond the needs of your family budget. It can be freely given to meet the burdens God places on your heart. God gives the surplus, but it is your responsibility to be in a position to recognize it. Only when you live on a budget plan will you be able to identify a surplus. Without a budget plan, not only is regular giving a strain, but all giving will feel like a sacrifice.

The Sacrifice

With the example of the widow's offering, Jesus teaches his disciples about sacrificial giving as compared to giving from surplus.

Jesus sat down opposite the place where the offerings were put and watched the crowd putting their money into the temple treasury. Many rich people threw in large amounts. But a poor widow came and put in two very small copper coins, worth only a few cents.

Calling his disciples to him, Jesus said, "Truly I tell you, this poor widow has put more into the treasury than all the others. They all gave out of their wealth; but she, out of her poverty, put in everything—all she had to live on" (Mark 12:41-44 NIV).

God owns it all! You give a regular gift to acknowledge that fact. The offering is a first step in opening a door to blessings and into a wonderful relationship with the Lord. Why would the Christian settle for eternal life when God is offering the abundant life NOW through His blessings?

The thief comes only in order to steal, kill, and destroy. I have come in order that you might have life—life in all its fullness (John 10:10 GNT).

You must remember that everything you have, even the ability to produce it, comes from God:

But remember the Lord your God, for it is he who gives you the ability to produce wealth, and so confirms his covenant, which he swore to your ancestors, as it is today (Deuteronomy 8:18 NIV).

John answered, "No one can have anything unless God gives it" (John 3:27 GNT).

Who made you superior to others? Didn't God give you everything you have? Well, then, how can you boast, as if what you have were not a gift? (1 Corinthians 4:7 GNT).

By ourselves we are not qualified in any way to claim that we can do anything. Rather, God makes us qualified (2 Corinthians 3:5 GW).

The blessings are great for those who give a regular gift (a tithe) from the first fruits of their labors. The blessings are even greater for those who give additionally from their surplus. But as Jesus so clearly illustrated, the blessings are the *greatest* for those with the faith and trust that allow them to give out of sacrifice. Remember, the blessing is in the attitude, not the money. God knows your heart when you give.

Beyond the Money

Once you are freed from the bondage of money, you will begin to see the great dichotomy of the spiritual life: You gain more when you give more. Jesus teaches this principle over and over.

Another great principle is that of sowing and reaping. *Remember this: Whoever sows sparingly will also reap sparingly, and whoever sows generously will also reap generously* (2 Corinthians 9:6 NIV). It is a principle that applies to more than just money.

One of God's blessings is the joy and the privilege He gives you to help others in their time of need. *I am not trying to relieve others by putting a burden on you; but since you have plenty at this time, it is only fair that you should help those who are in need. Then, when you are in need and they have plenty, they will help you. In this way both are treated equally* (2 Corinthians 8:14 GNT).

God desires that we have a balanced attitude toward material things. *Keep falsehood and lies far from me; give me neither poverty nor riches, but give me only my daily bread. Otherwise, I may have too much and disown you and say, "Who is the Lord?" Or I may become poor and steal, and so dishonor the name of my God* (Proverbs 30:8-9 NIV).

PART THREE
Assimilation

Chapter Seven
Long-Term Planning

In this last section of *Solving the Money Puzzle*, the three chapters address areas of life that can only be mastered with an on-going desire for wisdom. To successfully deal with the three topics (Long-Term Planning, Teaching Children, and Government), wisdom must overcome emotion. God's Word provides you with the wisdom you will need, but you must *assimilate* it. Assimilate is defined: *to learn something so that it is fully understood and can be used.*

Should a Christian invest money in the stock market? Is it wrong to accumulate a surplus? Does the Bible teach that wealth and riches are evil?

Long-term planning includes things such as elimination of debt, insurance, retirement, education, investments, wills and burial plans. God expects the Christian to be a responsible steward in all of these areas. Every area of your life must be an example of excellence and orderliness, including long-term planning. Then you will be free to call upon the Lord in times of trouble outside of our control.

Check your Motive

God's Word teaches that you should look ahead and identify future needs, and plan for them. The problem comes when you cross the line that divides *need* from *greed*. Without a long-term plan, not only will you be unable to provide for yourself and your family, but it will be extremely difficult to do God's work.

What about the stock market? There are those who equate investing in the stock market to gambling. There are differences, however, between gambling at a casino or buying lottery tickets, and buying stock. Gamblers risk money in hopes of "luck" rewarding them with a quick gain. Wise investors buy partial ownership in companies in the hopes of making money over time, which can be a sound way to plan for the future. The difference really comes down to the motive or the intent. As long as you honor your financial commitments to God and your family, and maintain a spirit of generosity and thankfulness, investing is an option Christians can consider. *Committed and persistent work pays off; get-rich-quick schemes are ripoffs* (Proverbs 28:20 MSG).

You've heard the saying: You will never see a hearse towing a U-Haul. This saying emphasized the foolishness of hoarding and greed. Paul, the aged and experienced apostle, writes to the young pastor Timothy who was facing a heavy burden of responsibility in the church at Ephesus. Paul warned Timothy to be on his guard and to avoid greedy motives. While encouraging him to pursue godliness with contentment, Paul said, *For we brought nothing into the world, and we can take nothing out of it* (1 Timothy 6:7 NIV).

Again, we see this principle in the following verse: *Surely everyone goes around like a mere phantom; in vain they rush about, heaping up wealth without knowing whose it will finally be* (Psalm 39:6 NIV).

The Christian is best able to plan for the future when he accepts his position as a *steward* rather than an *owner*. Then the motive for his plans will be established with the right attitude, and his labor will be fruitful. *No matter how much a lazy person may want something, he will never get it. A hard worker will get everything he wants* (Proverbs 13:4 NIV).

You are responsible to manage what God has given you (small or large). When you fail to do your part by not planning for the future, you become like the lazy person and end up with nothing. *A farmer too lazy to plow his fields at the right time will have nothing to harvest* (Proverbs 20:4 GNT).

Webster defines "prudent" as, *exercising sound judgment in practical matters*; *cautious in conduct, not rash*; *managing carefully*.

Scripture teaches that prudent men do four things:

1) Act with knowledge: *All who are prudent act with knowledge, but fools expose their folly* (Proverbs 13:16 GNT).

2) Gives thought to their ways: *The wisdom of the prudent is to give thought to their ways, but the folly of fools is deception* (Proverbs 14:8 NIV).

The simple believe anything, but the prudent give thought to their steps (Proverbs 14:15 NIV).

3) Are crowned with knowledge: *The simple inherit folly, but the prudent are crowned with knowledge* (Proverbs 14:18 NIV).

4) Sees danger and takes refuge: *The prudent see danger and take refuge, but the simple keep going and pay the penalty* (Proverbs 27:12 NIV).

When it comes to planning for the future, we can learn a lot from one of God's smallest creatures. *Lazy people should learn a lesson from the way ants live. They have no leader, chief, or ruler, but they store up their food during the summer, getting ready for winter* (Proverbs 6:6-8 GNT).

Every Christian needs to address the different aspects of long-term planning. In doing so, you exemplify an attitude of orderliness and excellence. The critical aspect of your planning is your motive. Let your plans be a result of known future financial needs rather than insatiable greed.

Plan your Method

The goal of the Christian in long-term financial planning should be to get into a position to better be able to serve without having to be pressured with the "daily grind." Due to the destructive power of inflation, long-term planning is essential.

Every method of investing has risk associated with it. Typically, the greater the potential return, the greater the probable risk. In all of your investment planning, God's principles will keep you safe.

After the establishment of an emergency fund (approximately three-to-six times your monthly expenses), the wisest use of your surplus savings is to free yourself from all consumer debt (debt on things that go down in value). The next step would be to consider a method of long-term investing for retirement or college funding.

Diversification (don't put all your eggs in one basket) is an important Biblical principle to consider when putting your savings at risk: *Invest in seven ventures, yes, in eight; you do not know what disaster may come upon the land* (Ecclesiastes 11:2 NIV).

Also, take time to seek advice from those you respect. *Get all the advice you can, and you will succeed; without it you will fall* (Proverbs 15:22 GNT). And never invest in something you don't understand well enough to explain it to your spouse or a friend in such a way that they can understand it. In other words, don't be *sold* an investment.

When you invest, it is your responsibility, as a steward of God's money, to ensure that the investment is ethical. *It is better to have a little, honestly earned, than to have a large income, dishonestly gained* (Proverbs 16:8 GNT).

Is a Surplus Unscriptural?

Many Christians mistakenly believe that it is wrong to accumulate a surplus. As you have seen, this is only the case when your motive is one of greed and hoarding. Saving for known future needs is a part of being a wise steward.

Some Christians also believe that it is unspiritual for a Christian to be wealthy. This too is not true. It is not the amount we are given to manage that is important. What is important is what we do with what we are given to manage.

The Parable of the Talents

In the *Parable of the Talents,* each servant was given a portion of their master's wealth to manage. The portion they were each given was *according to his ability.*

I once read that at the time of the parable, a day's wage was equivalent to $32, and each portion that was given to the servants would have equaled $5.7 million (gold), or $384,000 (silver). It should be noted that although each of the three servants was entrusted to manage a very large amount of his master's wealth, Jesus never insinuated that the amount was an issue of concern. The main lesson to be learned from this parable is the importance of being a wise manager of whatever God has decided to give you to manage—regardless of its value.

"Again, it will be like a man going on a journey, who called his servants and entrusted his wealth to them. To one he gave five bags of gold, to another two bags, and to another one bag, each according to his ability. Then he went on his journey.

"The man who had received five bags of gold went at once and put his money to work and gained five bags more. So also, the

one with two bags of gold gained two more. But the man who had received one bag went off, dug a hole in the ground and hid his master's money.

"After a long time the master of those servants returned and settled accounts with them. The man who had received five bags of gold brought the other five. 'Master,' he said, 'you entrusted me with five bags of gold. See, I have gained five more.'

"His master replied, 'Well done, good and faithful servant! You have been faithful with a few things; I will put you in charge of many things. Come and share your master's happiness!'

"The man with two bags of gold also came. 'Master,' he said, 'you entrusted me with two bags of gold; see, I have gained two more.' "His master replied, 'Well done, good and faithful servant! You have been faithful with a few things; I will put you in charge of many things. Come and share your master's happiness!'" (Matthew 25:14-23 NIV).

Another example in scripture that shows us that wealth is not evil or unscriptural is seen when God asked Solomon what he wanted.

At Gibeon the Lord appeared to Solomon during the night in a dream, and God said, *"Ask for whatever you want me to give you"* (I Kings 3:5 NIV).

Solomon replied: *So give your servant a discerning heart to govern your people and to distinguish between right and wrong* (1 Kings 3:9 NIV).

This pleased God. *So God said to him, "Since you have asked for this and not for long life or wealth for yourself, nor have asked for the death of your enemies but for discernment in administering justice, I will do what you have asked. I will give you a wise and discerning heart, so that there will never have been anyone like you, nor will there ever be. Moreover, I will give you what you have not asked for—both wealth and honor—so that in your lifetime you will have no equal among king* (1 Kings 3:11-13 NIV).

Solomon chose wisdom (the understanding to discern judgment) over everything else, and God gave him wisdom, honor, and wealth—wealth greater than any king that lived during Solomon's lifetime.

We also see that Job was given great wealth by God. *After Job had prayed for his friends, the Lord restored his fortunes and gave him twice as much as he had before* (Job 42:10 NIV).

It is obvious, by these and other passages, that in God's eyes, riches and wealth are not a problem. The problem occurs when you have the wrong attitude toward money.

Serve your Master

Jesus said, *"No one can serve two masters. Either you will hate the one and love the other, or you will be devoted to the one and despise the other. You cannot serve both God and money"* (Matthew 6:24 NIV).

When money is our master, it becomes our sole purpose in life and our greatest love. When our motive for long-term financial planning is solely to build a surplus, you are hoarding. On the other hand, when you are negligent in planning for long-term financial needs, you are irresponsible and not prudent.

God has given clear principles that will guide us in the practical matters of life. You will always find His blessings when you live according to those principles.

In addition, the Christian has a higher calling than to spend our lives muddled among those whose master is money. This life is like a vapor. *For what is your life? It is even a vapour, that appeareth for a little time, and then vanisheth away* (James 4:14 KJV).

The greatest investment that the Christian can ever make is in the things with lasting eternal value.

Do not store up for yourselves treasures on earth, where moths and vermin destroy, and where thieves break in and steal. But store up for yourselves treasures in heaven, where moths and vermin do not destroy, and where thieves do not break in and steal. For where your treasure is, there your heart will be also (Matthew 6:19-21 NIV).

In his old age, David made an observation of the heirs of a righteous man. *Once I was young, and now I am old. Yet I have never seen the godly abandoned or their children begging for bread* (Psalm 37:25 NLT).

More important than money is the spiritual inheritance that you leave your children. *Good people leave an inheritance to their grandchildren, but the sinner's wealth passes to the godly* (Proverbs 13:22 NLT).

Long-term planning is the responsibility of every Christian. If you are married, you need to set aside a time to discuss each area of concern with your spouse—everything from debt to burial plans. A life of orderliness and excellence is God's standard for the Christian.

Chapter Eight
Teaching Children about Money

When it comes to earning, spending, saving and giving money, who has the greatest influence on your children? What is the most *efficient* way to teach your children about money? What is the most *effective* way to teach your children about money?

One of the greatest concerns of the Christian parent should be that their children understand and apply the wisdom of the Lord in regard to personal money management. With the wrong attitude about money, children are often trapped by the prevailing mindset of the secular society and forfeit the blessings of a productive life of service for the Lord.

As Christian parents, God appoints you as temporary stewards and guardians of *His* children. He has given you the great responsibility to train and equip them to be prepared for service for Him. Proper training of your children is one of your greatest ways of investing in the future work of the Lord.

Train up a child in the way he should go: and when he is old, he will not depart from it (Proverbs 22:6 KJV).

Teaching by Example

Teaching your children is nothing more than the transfer of wisdom (your understanding of God's principles), to them. When you are living a life of obedience, orderliness, and excellence before your children, you are teaching them by example. It doesn't matter what you *say*, your children will eventually see the convictions of your heart in what you *do*.

The following verses tell you what the prerequisites are for you to be an effective teacher. It then tells you how and when to teach your children.

Love the Lord your God with all your heart and with all your soul and with all your strength. These commandments that I give you today are to be on your hearts. Impress them on your children. Talk about them when you sit at home and when you walk along the road, when you lie down and when you get up (Deuteronomy 6:5-7 NIV).

God's Word puts the primary responsibility on the parent(s) to carefully teach their children about all of the issues of life— including money. However, you can only effectively teach what you believe and understand.

The time that you are given to prepare your children is very brief. You will not be held responsible for their decisions, but rather for the way you teach and train them. In other words, you are not responsible for the "outcome" only the "input". Your children are God's creation. He has a specific purpose for their lives. He shaped them in the womb for a purpose that only they can fulfill.

Biblical principles regarding the practical matters concerning money management will give your children a solid foundation upon which to establish their lives. You must teach your children that God owns it all and we are stewards (managers). You must also instruct and mentor your children in the practical areas of money management. *The godly walk with integrity; blessed are their children who follow them* (Proverbs 20:7 NLT).

The spiritual inheritance that God has given you is the greatest thing you can pass on to your children.

...things we have heard and known, things our ancestors have told us. We will not hide them from their descendants; we will tell the next generation the praiseworthy deeds of the Lord, his power, and the wonders he has done. He decreed statutes for Jacob and established the law in Israel, which he commanded our ancestors to teach their children, so the next generation would know them, even the children yet to be born, and they in turn would tell their children (Psalm 78:3-6 NIV).

The blessings of sound teaching do not stop in the lives of your children, they are passed on to the generations that follow. *But from everlasting to everlasting the Lord's love is with those who fear him, and his righteousness with their children's children* (Psalm 103:17, 18 NIV).

If your descendants obey the terms of my covenant and the laws that I teach them, then your royal line will continue forever and ever (Psalm 132:12 NIV).

Children's children are a crown to the aged, and parents are the pride of their children (Proverbs 17:6 NIV).

There are many oil producing trees mentioned in the Bible. The best oil was obtained from the green olive fruit of the olive tree. It was used for several things:

Fuel for lamps—*Command the people of Israel to bring you pure oil of pressed olives for the light, to keep the lamps burning continually* (Exodus 27:20 NLT).

As anointing oil—*When you present grain as an offering to the Lord, the offering must consist of choice flour. You are to pour olive oil on it...* (Leviticus 2:1 NIV).

As an article of commerce—*In return, Solomon sent him an annual payment of 100,000 bushels of wheat for his household and 110,000 gallons of pure olive oil* (1 Kings 5:11 NLT).

For dressing wounds—*He went to him and bandaged his wounds, pouring on oil and wine* (Luke 10:34 NIV).

The olive tree stood about 20 feet tall with a gnarled, twisted trunk, white flowers, and berries that ripen to a black color. The olive tree grew slowly and continued to bear fruit after reaching a great age. A very interesting characteristic of the tree was that, before it died, new branches sprouted from its roots. It is a wonderful example that is seen in the following passage of scripture.

In Psalms, you see a man who walks in the ways of the Lord. He is able to provide for his family and you can assume that he has his financial house in order. Notice the references to his children.

Blessed are all who fear the Lord, who walk in obedience to him. You will eat the fruit of your labor; blessings and prosperity will be yours. Your wife will be like a fruitful vine within your house; your children will be like olive shoots around your table. Yes, this will be the blessing for the man who fears the Lord. May the Lord bless you from Zion; may you see the prosperity of Jerusalem all the days of your life. May you live to see your children's children—peace be on Israel (Psalm 128:1-6 NIV).

Because of this man's life being an example to his children, his children are able to teach their children, and the generations to follow will be blessed. Just as the olive tree continues to bear fruit in its old age and sprout new branches before it's death, so will the children of a man be who walks in the wisdom of God's Word.

As referenced earlier: *The godly walk with integrity; blessed are their children who follow them* (Proverbs 20:7 NIV).

Teaching in Love

Many parents and grandparents mistakenly shower their children and grandchildren with gifts in the name of love. With the beginning of every tear is the promise of the purchase of an item that the parent hopes will serve to pacify the child's demands.

If you love your children and desire to see them grow up to become wise managers of their financial affairs, you must be willing to take the time required to teach them and train them. Children need boundaries to feel safe. They need to be guided, instructed, and trained in the differences between right and wrong. They need to be taught how to respect and love others. Children cannot be expected to learn this principle on their own, or from society, or in school. God has entrusted the parents with the primary responsibility of teaching their children. *For the Lord corrects those he loves, just as a father corrects a child in whom he delights* (Proverbs 3:12 NLT).

Children that are left to run wild like animals are not loved and become a detriment to society. Undisciplined children do not grow in wisdom, and they have difficulty adapting to the strain and stress of life. They often resort to evil measures, and they have difficulty finding their purpose in life. They are a disgrace to their mother. *To discipline a child produces wisdom, but a mother is disgraced by an undisciplined child* (Proverbs 29:15 NLT).

Discipline comes in many forms. Discipline is used to channel the child's natural tendency towards foolishness. *Those who spare the rod of discipline hate their children. Those who love their children care enough to discipline them* (Proverbs 13:24 NLT).

When you refrain from teaching your children by not correcting them, you do them no good. *A youngster's heart is filled with foolishness, but physical discipline will drive it far away* (Proverbs 22:15 NLT).

All teaching and correction requires an abundance of love. When you correct your child with anger, you provoke them to wrath. *Fathers, do not provoke your children to anger by the way you treat them. Rather, bring them up with the discipline and instruction that comes from the Lord* (Ephesians 6:4 NLT).

Teaching with Hope

The Bible is filled with hope for those who train and teach their children properly. Your life, their lives, and the lives of their children are promised to be blessed by God. There is but a short time in the lives of your children that you can effectively teach them. You must take advantage of every opportunity.

Impress them on your children. Talk about them when you sit at home and when you walk along the road, when you lie down and when you get up (Deuteronomy 6:7 NIV).

It is with the hope found in God's Word that you must continue. *Discipline your children, for in that there is hope* (Proverbs 19:18 NIV).

Your greatest hope as a Christian parent is that your children will bring you joy as a result of your training them in the ways of the Lord. *Discipline your children, and they will give you peace of mind and will make your heart glad* (Proverbs 29:17 NLT).

You must also continually encourage your children. Set before them dreams and goals worthy of striving for, giving them hope. Help them discover the special purpose that God has created for them. Teach them the value of wisdom over intelligence. Make them aware of how much God loves them.

The most *efficient* way for you to train your children (producing the desired results with a minimum of effort) is by example.

The most *effective* way for you to train your children is in love. Teaching your children *by example* and *in love* will return the greatest investment of your time.

There is always hope for your children when you do all you can to teach, train, and correct them as God has instructed in His Word.

Children are a gift from the Lord; they are a reward from Him (Psalm 127:3 NLT).

Chapter Nine

Government – Friend or Foe?

What perspective should Christians have towards human authority? Should Christians pay taxes? What level of responsibility does government have in meeting the basic needs of society?

To some, the government is perceived as an enemy who, without adequate justification, is continually imposing excessive legislation and taxation that results in personal hardship and the loss of quality of life.

To others, the government is perceived as a lifeline which offers the opportunity of hope for both the present and the future. Both perceptions are driven by money: What is the government taking from me? What can the government give me?

Your perception of what financial role the government should play in your life is a good indicator as to whether you have accepted your position as God's steward. As a steward (*manager*), you understand God's purpose for government and your relationship to it.

As an owner, you become blinded to God's sovereignty because of your love of money. You forget that God ordains all authority. Throughout history there have been evil rulers and good rulers, but always the same God. A Christian is to obey his/her "master," "ruler," "government" (or any other name that is used for an established authority) unless the ruling authority instructs the Christian to do something that is in direct disobedience to God's Word.

Even when a government is oppressive, unfair, or unjust, the Christian should still live in obedience to authority and pray.

However, if my people, who are called by my name, will humble themselves, pray, search for me, and turn from their evil ways, then I will hear their prayer from heaven, forgive their sins, and heal their country. (2 Chronicles 7:14 GW).

God and Government

The purpose of a government, as instituted by God, is to provide individual nations with order and stability. This is possible through the implementation of laws and the enforcement of those laws. God intended for laws to enhance individual freedom (especially the freedom to accept or reject Christ), not restrict it. God intends for government to provide an environment of protection to those that desire to live in accordance with His will.

Nationalism vs. Internationalism

God's plan for order and stability is for individual nations to be ruled by independent national governments. The current movement towards internationalism (the governing of more than one nation or religion under one head) is in direct opposition to God's plan for continued freedom.

The *Tower of Babel* was a prime example of man's rebellion against God. It was an effort to create political and religious internationalism. As a result of man's rebellion and revolt, God saw the need to place division among the people. Read the story of the *Tower of Babel* and see if you can locate the two ways that God divided the people.

The Tower of Babel

Now the whole world had one language and a common speech. As people moved eastward, they found a plain in Shinar and settled there.

They said to each other, "Come, let's make bricks and bake them thoroughly." They used brick instead of stone, and tar for mortar. Then they said, "Come, let us build ourselves a city, with a tower that reaches to the heavens, so that we may make a name for ourselves; otherwise we will be scattered over the face of the whole earth."

But the Lord came down to see the city and the tower the people were building. The Lord said, "If as one people speaking the same language they have begun to do this, then nothing they plan to do will be impossible for them. Come, let us go down and confuse their language so they will not understand each other."

So the Lord scattered them from there over all the earth, and they stopped building the city. That is why it was called Babel—because there the Lord confused the language of the whole world. From there the Lord scattered them over the face of the whole earth (Genesis 11:1-9 NIV).

No form of internationalism is acceptable to God. This includes political internationalism (Communism, Socialism, One World Government, United Nations, etc.) and religious internationalism (Roman Catholic Church, the World Council of Churches, etc.) Christianity is 100% opposed to any form of internationalism.

When the Most High gave the nations their inheritance, when he divided all mankind, he set up boundaries for the peoples according to the number of the sons of Israel (Deuteronomy 32:8 NIV).

From one man he made all the nations, that they should inhabit the whole earth; and he marked out their appointed times in history and the boundaries of their lands (Acts 17:26 NIV).

There is a god of this world. He is sometimes referred to as the prince of this world. He is the enemy to all that is good and all that comes from God. He blinds the minds of those who live in darkness. But in time, he will be cast out.

The time for judging this world has come, when Satan, the ruler of this world, will be cast out (John 12:31 NLT);

I will not say much more to you, for the prince of this world is coming. He has no hold over me (John 14:30 NIV).

For if the gospel we preach is hidden, it is hidden only from those who are being lost. They do not believe, because their minds have been kept in the dark by the evil god of this world. He keeps them from seeing the light shining on them, the light that comes from the Good News about the glory of Christ, who is the exact likeness of God (2 Corinthians 4:3-4 GNT).

Internationalism (multiple nations under the leadership of one head) makes easy prey for the god of this world. On a smaller scale, the same detrimental effects can result when a national government tries to take control of the state. (For example: nationally controlled and mandated education)

When people are blinded by the god of this world, they willfully support his schemes. In the end, the people will see the consequences of their own foolish decisions and cry out for mercy when they suffer the oppression of the evil that has come upon them.

He will take your best fields, vineyards, and olive groves, and give them to his officials. He will take a tenth of your grain and of your grapes for his court officers and other officials. He will take your servants and your best cattle and donkeys, and make them work for him. He will take a tenth of your flocks. And you yourselves will become his slaves. When that time comes, you will complain bitterly because of your king, whom you yourselves chose, but the Lord will not listen to your complaints" (1 Samuel 8:14-18 GNT).

King Jehoiakim collected a tax from the people in proportion to their wealth, in order to raise the amount needed to pay the tribute demanded by the king of Egypt (2 Kings 23:35 GNT).

Others were saying, "We are mortgaging our fields, our vineyards and our homes to get grain during the famine." Still others were saying, "We have had to borrow money to pay the king's tax on our fields and vineyards" (Nehemiah 5:3-4 NIV).

God ordained government as a necessary part of His plan, and it takes money to run a government. Keeping law and order takes money. Certain privileges enjoyed in a nation takes money (highways, park system, etc.). Elected government leaders need to be supported (it is a full time job). Bona fide welfare takes money.

You and Government

Taxes are the greatest single concern to most Americans in regard to their relationship with government. In the following passages, read what Jesus taught about taxes.

When Jesus and his disciples came to Capernaum, the collectors of the Temple tax came to Peter and asked, "Does your teacher pay the Temple tax?"

"Of course," Peter answered.

When Peter went into the house, Jesus spoke up first, "Simon, what is your opinion? Who pays duties or taxes to the kings of this world? The citizens of the country or the foreigners?"

"The foreigners," answered Peter.

"Well, then," replied Jesus, "that means that the citizens don't have to pay. But we don't want to offend these people. So go to the lake and drop in a line. Pull up the first fish you hook, and in its mouth you will find a coin worth enough for my Temple tax and yours. Take it and pay them our taxes" (Matthew 17:24-27 GNT).

Tell us then, what is your opinion? Is it right to pay the

130

imperial tax to Caesar or not?"

But Jesus, knowing their evil intent, said, "You hypocrites, why are you trying to trap me? Show me the coin used for paying the tax." They brought him a denarius, and he asked them, "Whose image is this? And whose inscription?"

"Caesar's," they replied.

Then he said to them, "So give back to Caesar what is Caesar's, and to God what is God's" (Matthew 22:17-21 NIV).

At the time of Jesus' birth, Caesar Augustus was ruler of the Roman Empire. It was during the golden age of Rome. For more than 1,000 years, the land promised by God to the Israelites had been a battleground. The mighty empire built by Caesar Augustus was financed by the most sophisticated system of taxation the world had ever known. A periodic census was required to implement this system.

The story of Joseph and Mary offer an excellent example of how important it is for us to obey government. I think we are safe to assume that Joseph considered the taxes required by Rome to be excessive. However, in obedience, he traveled five days with a pregnant wife from Nazareth to Bethlehem to pay his taxes to Rome. If it had not been for his obedience to the Roman law, prophecy of Jesus' birth would not have been fulfilled.

In those days Caesar Augustus issued a decree that a census should be taken of the entire Roman world. (This was the first census that took place while Quirinius was governor of Syria.) And everyone went to their own town to register.

So Joseph also went up from the town of Nazareth in Galilee to Judea, to Bethlehem the town of David, because he belonged to the house and line of David. He went there to register with Mary, who was pledged to be married to him and was expecting a child. While they were there, the time came for the baby to be born, and she gave birth to her firstborn, a son. She wrapped him in cloths and placed him in a manger, because there was no guest room available for them (Luke 2:1-7 NIV).

Our Relationship with Those in Authority

The following passages of scripture outline the relationship we must have with government officials, and where these officials ultimately get their authority.

Let everyone be subject to the governing authorities, for there is

132

no authority except that which God has established. The authorities that exist have been established by God. Consequently, whoever rebels against the authority is rebelling against what God has instituted, and those who do so will bring judgment on themselves. For rulers hold no terror for those who do right, but for those who do wrong.

Do you want to be free from fear of the one in authority? Then do what is right and you will be commended. For the one in authority is God's servant for your good. But if you do wrong, be afraid, for rulers do not bear the sword for no reason. They are God's servants, agents of wrath to bring punishment on the wrongdoer. Therefore, it is necessary to submit to the authorities, not only because of possible punishment but also as a matter of conscience.

This is also why you pay taxes, for the authorities are God's servants, who give their full time to governing. Give to everyone what you owe them: If you owe taxes, pay taxes; if revenue, then revenue; if respect, then respect; if honor, then honor (Romans 13:1-7 NIV).

Submit yourselves for the Lord's sake to every human authority: whether to the emperor, as the supreme authority, or to governors, who are sent by him to punish those who do wrong and to commend those who do right. For it is God's will that by doing good you should silence the ignorant talk of foolish people. Live as free people, but do not use your freedom as a cover-up for evil; live as God's slaves. Show proper respect to everyone, love the family of believers, fear God, honor the emperor (1 Peter 2:13-17 NIV).

Government is necessary and plays a vital role in the life of every Christian. It is therefore the responsibility of every Christian to take an active part in the governing process. Only with the right *attitude* can your voice be effective in helping to hold the government accountable to God's purpose.

Government as a Provider

When government leaders attempt to change the role of the government from that of *protector* to *provider*, the results will be a loss of individual freedom and, ultimately, economic collapse.

Because of the original sin of Adam and Eve, God made it clear from the beginning that we would be required to work hard for our food.

And he said to the man, "You listened to your wife and ate the fruit which I told you not to eat. Because of what you have done, the ground will be under a curse. You will have to work hard all your life to make it produce enough food for you. It will produce weeds and thorns, and you will have to eat wild plants. You will have to work hard and sweat to make the soil produce anything, until you go back to the soil from which you were formed. You were made from soil, and you will become soil again" (Genesis 3:17-19 GNT).

Universal social welfare and scheming to find a way for the government to become a provider to those without legitimate needs was not a part of God's plan. However, instruction from God's Word does speak strongly to us about the individual responsibility to provide for our families and dependent widows. Paul makes the Christian work ethic abundantly clear: *But if any do not take care of their relatives, especially the members of their own family, they have denied the faith and are worse than an unbeliever* (1 Timothy 5:8 GNT).

But if any Christian woman has widows in her family, she must take care of them and not put the burden on the church, so that it may take care of the widows who are all alone (1 Timothy 5:16 GNT).

When you don't work, it results in idleness. It encourages the attitude: *The world owes me a living*. Paul had some strong words about those who are lazy and refuse to work.

While we were with you, we used to tell you, "Whoever refuses to work is not allowed to eat." We say this because we hear that there are some people among you who live lazy lives and who do nothing except meddle in other people's business. In the name of the Lord Jesus Christ we command these people and warn them to lead orderly lives and work to earn their own living (2 Thessalonians 3:10-12 GNT).

You develop God's attitude in relation to your finances when you transfer complete ownership to Him. Only then can you see God's design to meet the genuine needs of those around you.

I am not trying to relieve others by putting a burden on you; but since you have plenty at this time, it is only fair that you should help those who are in need. Then, when you are in need and they have plenty, they will help you. In this way both are treated equally (2 Corinthians 8:14 GNT).

Corruption in the government could be minimized if those responsible for the distribution of finances to the needy were godly men and women filled with faith and wisdom. When the apostles were faced with the needs of the people, they ordered a group of godly men to be appointed and given the responsibility of determining who should qualify for partial or full financial assistance.

Some time later, as the number of disciples kept growing, there was a quarrel between the Greek-speaking Jews and the native Jews. The Greek-speaking Jews claimed that their widows were being neglected in the daily distribution of funds. So the twelve apostles called the whole group of believers together and said, "It is not right for us to neglect the preaching of God's word in order to handle finances. So then, friends, choose seven men among you who are known to be full of the Holy Spirit and wisdom, and we will put them in charge of this matter. We ourselves, then, will give our full time to prayer and the work of preaching."

The whole group was pleased with the apostles' proposal, so they chose Stephen, a man full of faith and the Holy Spirit, and Philip, Prochorus, Nicanor, Timon, Parmenas, and Nicolaus, a Gentile from Antioch who had earlier been converted to Judaism. The group presented them to the apostles, who prayed and placed their hands on them.

And so the word of God continued to spread. The number of disciples in Jerusalem grew larger and larger, and a great number of priests accepted the faith (Acts 6:1-7 GNT).

Note: Just because a woman had lost her husband, it did not automatically qualify her to receive benefits as a widow. There were certain requirements before a woman was considered a widow: *Do not add any widow to the list of widows unless she is over sixty years of age. In addition, she must have been married only once* (1 Timothy 5:9 GNT).

Just as is seen in the following story, our busy schedules often keep us from hearing God's voice calling us to love others when they are in need?

Jesus answered, "There was once a man who was going down from Jerusalem to Jericho when robbers attacked him, stripped him, and beat him up, leaving him half dead. It so happened that a priest was going down that road; but when he saw the man, he walked on by on the other side. In the same way a Levite also came there, went over and looked at the man, and then walked on by on the other side.

"But a Samaritan who was traveling that way came upon the

man, and when he saw him, his heart was filled with pity. He went over to him, poured oil and wine on his wounds and bandaged them; then he put the man on his own animal and took him to an inn, where he took care of him. The next day he took out two silver coins and gave them to the innkeeper. 'Take care of him,' he told the innkeeper, 'and when I come back this way, I will pay you whatever else you spend on him.'"

And Jesus concluded, "In your opinion, which one of these three acted like a neighbor toward the man attacked by the robbers?"

The teacher of the Law answered, "The one who was kind to him."

Jesus replied, "You go, then, and do the same" (Luke 10:30-37 GNT).

Jesus tells another story:

And Jesus said to his disciples, "Suppose one of you should go to a friend's house at midnight and say, 'Friend, let me borrow three loaves of bread. A friend of mine who is on a trip has just come to my house, and I don't have any food for him!' And suppose your friend should answer from inside, 'Don't bother me! The door is already locked, and my children and I are in bed. I can't get up and give you anything.' Well, what then? I tell you that even if he will not get up and give you the bread because you are his friend, yet he will get up and give you everything you need because you are not ashamed to keep on asking.

"And so I say to you: Ask, and you will receive; seek, and you will find; knock, and the door will be opened to you. For those who ask will receive, and those who seek will find, and the door will be opened to anyone who knocks (Luke 11:5-10 GNT).

Over one-half of the United States Government's budget is spent on individual benefits such as Social Security, Medicare, Medicaid, federal retirement, unemployment, food stamps, family support, SSI, and veterans benefits. If you include the state and local grants, the total amount spent on benefit programs in the United States would total nearly two-thirds of the annual budget. These percentages are growing every year.

The abuse of welfare can easily destroy a nation. Welfare is abused when it promotes an attitude of mental laziness, promotes a lack of initiative, and promotes a "society owes me a living" mentality. The Founders understood well the dangers of welfare programs and redistribution schemes.

Benjamin Franklin said: *"I am for doing good to the poor, but I differ in opinion of the means. I think the best way of doing good to the poor, is not making them easy in poverty, but leading or driving them out of it. In my youth I travelled much, and I observed in different countries, that the more public provisions were made for the poor, the less they provided for themselves, and of course became poorer. And, on the contrary, the less was done for them, the more they did for themselves, and became richer."*

And James Madison, the author of the Constitution, told the House of Representatives that welfare is not the duty of the Federal government. *"The government of the United States is a definite government, confined to specified objects. It is not like the state governments, whose powers are more general. Charity is no part of the legislative duty of the government."*

As a Christian, you need to actively encourage your government officials and hold them accountable to God's purpose for government. Support those who are willing to stand strong in their compliance with Biblical principles. You need to be the salt of the earth. *You are like salt for the whole human race. But if salt loses its saltiness, there is no way to make it salty again. It has become worthless, so it is thrown out and people trample on it* (Matthew 5:13 GNT).

God does not exclude any person. He loves us all equally and desires that we all spend eternity with Him in Heaven.

First of all, then, I urge that petitions, prayers, requests, and thanksgivings be offered to God for all people; for kings and all others who are in authority, that we may live a quiet and peaceful life with all reverence toward God and with proper conduct. This is good and it pleases God our Savior, who wants everyone to be saved and to come to know the truth (1 Timothy 2:1-4 GNT).

When is a Nation Blessed?

Blessed is the nation whose God is the Lord, the people he chose for his inheritance (Psalm 33:12 NIV).

However, if my people, who are called by my name, will humble themselves, pray, search for me, and turn from their evil ways, then I will hear their prayer from heaven, forgive their sins, and heal their country (2 Chronicles 7:14 GW).

Even when you are not pleased with those in positions of authority, you have no need to be troubled. God is ultimately in control. *I help kings to govern and rulers to make good laws. Every ruler on earth governs with my help, officials and nobles alike* (Proverbs 8:15-16 GNT).

The Lord controls the mind of a king as easily as he directs the course of a stream (Proverbs 21:1 GNT).

God does have a purpose for government. You need to take seriously your Christian responsibility to pray for your leaders in government.

Elected government leaders (national, state, and local) need to be held accountable. They should support God's purpose for government as that of a *protector* not a *provider*. Encourage your government leaders to make decisions that would be in alignment with God's purposes.

Conclusion

What do you need to change in your life so that God is first in your finances?

Solving the Money Puzzle has covered many Biblical principles that should challenge your thinking concerning your attitude about money. What are you going to do with the challenge laid before you in God's Word?

"You should live in a way that proves you belong to the God who calls you into his kingdom and glory" (1 Thessalonians 2:12 GW).

Typically, you will respond in one of three ways after being confronted with a Biblical challenge.

You might meet the challenge head-on and begin fine-tuning

and making the necessary changes to start living a more surrendered life. As you do, your spiritual life will grow deeper roots that will secure you firmly in truth and wisdom. Then, when the rough winds come and somebody in your family gets sick or somebody dies or you have unexpected hardship, the trial doesn't' blow you away.

Or, after reading God's Word, you might initially get excited and commit to change. But you will soon get too busy and return to your defeated life. Your attempt to change was superficial, emotional, and impulsive, and it ultimately failed because you didn't give it time to soak in. Your spiritual roots remain in shallow soil making you vulnerable to upset with the slightest winds of trouble.

You might simply do nothing as a result of a heart that has become so hardened by the world that even the Words of the Living God no longer have any effect. Darkness has become your new normal.

Unless the Word of God pricks your heart, there will be no change in your life. You must confess the sin that deceives you from the truth and holds you captive. Only when you ask God for forgiveness can your heart be made pure. It is then, and only then, that you will see Him. *Blessed are the pure in heart, for they will see God* (Matthew 5:8 NIV).

What happens to the seeds of truth found in God's Word is totally dependent on you. Remember, a surrendered heart will always yield a fruitful life. You can't hear God if your mind is crowded with other thoughts or concerns—particularly worries, plans, and activities. You must eliminate the distractions if you want to hear God when He calls.

The Parable of the Sower and Soils

In the *Parable of the Sower and Soils*, Jesus presents an excellent illustration of how and why people respond differently to the Word of God.

People kept coming to Jesus from one town after another; and when a great crowd gathered, Jesus told this parable:

"Once there was a man who went out to sow grain. As he scattered the seed in the field, some of it fell along the path, where it was stepped on, and the birds ate it up. Some of it fell on rocky ground, and when the plants sprouted, they dried up because the soil had no moisture. Some of the seed fell among thorn bushes, which grew up with the plants and choked them.

147

And some seeds fell in good soil; the plants grew and bore grain, one hundred grains each."

And Jesus concluded, "Listen, then, if you have ears!"

The Purpose of Parables

His disciples asked Jesus what this parable meant, and he answered, "The knowledge of the secrets of the Kingdom of God has been given to you, but to the rest it comes by means of parables, so that they may look but not see, and listen but not understand.

Jesus Explains the Parable of the Sower and Soils

"This is what the parable means: the seed is the word of God. The seeds that fell along the path stand for those who hear; but the Devil comes and takes the message away from their hearts in order to keep them from believing and being saved. The seeds that fell on rocky ground stand for those who hear the message and receive it gladly. But it does not sink deep into them; they believe only for a while but when the time of testing comes, they fall away. The seeds that fell among thorn bushes stand for those who hear; but the worries and riches and pleasures of this life crowd in and choke them, and their fruit

never ripens. The seeds that fell in good soil stand for those who hear the message and retain it in a good and obedient heart, and they persist until they bear fruit (Luke 8:4-15 GNT).

This parable represents four attitudes. It is possible for you to experience all four attitudes in the same day. One moment you go, "God, I don't want to hear you, because I know what you're going to say." And the next moment you say, "Lord, tell me quick." Then you hear it and think it's good, but you don't do anything about it. Maybe the fruit starts to bear in your life, but then you get busy with your job or school or your kids, and the weeds grow up. Then other times you say, "God, whatever you want. I'm totally open to you."

God wants you to have an attitude of obedience so you can bear fruit — the biblical term for being successful. God wants you to be fruitful in your business, your family, your friendships, and your relationship with others.

The weeds and thorns in life grow automatically. You don't have to cultivate weeds. In fact, weeds are a sign of neglect. When you see a yard or garden overgrown with weeds, it tells you that the owner is not tending the yard or garden. The same is true for your spiritual life. Weeds in your spiritual life are a sign that you're neglecting time with God.

You can't hear God if you don't spend time with Him. As you consider what might be robbing you of your time with God, think about three of your greatest enemies:

Worry. Worries are weeds. The problems and pressures of daily living (the cares of the world) make it harder to hear God.

Riches. When you get so busy trying to make a living, pay your bills, and get out of debt, there is no time left for God.

Pleasure. There's nothing wrong with pleasure. But God said that when you're so busy pursuing fun, you miss Him and His plans and purpose for your life.

As you consider your personal response to the challenge of God's Word, meditate on these four passages of scripture:

Don't worry about anything; instead, pray about everything. Tell God what you need, and thank him for all he has done. Then you will experience God's peace, which exceeds anything we can understand. His peace will guard your hearts and minds as you live in Christ Jesus (Philippians 4:6-7 NLT).

For as he thinketh in his heart, so is he (Proverbs 23:7 KJV).

We demolish arguments and every pretension that sets itself up against the knowledge of God, and we take captive every thought to make it obedient to Christ (2 Corinthians 10:5 NIV).

If anyone, then, knows the good they ought to do and doesn't do it, it is sin for them (James 4:17 NIV).

If you feel overwhelmed or confused about a decision that you're trying to make, you're probably caught up in yourself and not God's voice. The Bible says, *God is not a God of disorder but of peace* (1 Corinthians 14:33a NIV). He is not the author of confusion. So if you're feeling confused, guess what? It's not God's voice speaking in your life.

Financial freedom became a reality for me when I discovered that the missing piece to the money puzzle was not simply more money, but, instead, my relationship with money. The same can happen for you.

I encourage you to make the Word of God your absolute for all of life, including your relationship with money. If you do, you will enjoy the wonderful blessings and freedom that God promises to all Christians. Remember: It's not about the money!

Books by Mike Coe

Fiction

Flight to Paradise (The Flight Trilogy – Book 1)

Flight into Darkness (The Flight Trilogy – Book 2)

Flight to Freedom (The Flight Trilogy – Book 3)

CoeBooks.com

www.ingramcontent.com/pod-product-compliance
Lightning Source LLC
Chambersburg PA
CBHW060929040426
42445CB00011B/862